An American Patriot's Journey
To **"Make America Great Again"**

A Veteran's Stand for Faith, Freedom,
and the Soul of America

By: Ron Coleman
aka Grey Wolf

Grey Wolf Press
An Independent American Publisher
GreyWolfPress.net

Printed in the United States of America

First Edition, 2025

ISBNs
Paperback: **979-8-9937521-2-9**
Hardcover: **979-8-9937521-7-4**

Cover Design: by the author
Interior Layout: by the author

Dedication

To President Donald J. Trump,

for inspiring a renewed belief that America's best days are still ahead.

To my supporters and moderators,

who stood with me mile after mile, keeping the message alive and the streams rolling— you are the heartbeat behind the mission.

To Bubba,

whose friendship and faith in this journey never wavered. You may be gone, brother, but your spirit rides every mile beside me.

To Mr. T,

who came running in a time of need, stood guard every mile, and drove *Beechy* with loyalty, grit, and faith. Your strength and quiet courage made the impossible possible.

And to my family,

for your patience, your love, and your understanding as I chased a calling bigger than myself. Every step I take is built on your strength.

Epigraph

"Freedom is never more than one generation away from extinction. We didn't pass it to our children in the bloodstream—it must be fought for, protected, and handed on."
— Ronald Reagan

* * *

And yet, the freedom I fight for began long before my first breath. There was only one entity in the room the day I was born—besides the doctors, the nurses, and my mother. That same one gave me my sight, my breath, my hearing, my life—and only He can take those things away.
— Ron Coleman, February 2022 Interview

FOREWORD

I first met Ron "Greywolf" Coleman through a YouTube live stream. I had been searching for news about The People's Convoy—a group of truckers traveling from Adelanto, California, to Washington, D.C., to voice their concerns about the COVID-19 mandates.

At first, I clicked through different drivers, curious but not invested. Then one voice stood out—he spoke calmly, knowledgeably, and from the heart about the Constitution, freedom, and responsibility. That voice belonged to Ron.

I watched as he and the other convoy members arrived in Washington, D.C., where they met with Senators Ted Cruz and Ron Johnson. Ron spoke clearly and with conviction about why they had come—the letters and drawings from children, the stories from families who had struggled through illness and uncertainty. His compassion and sincerity reached everyone listening.

A proud Air Force veteran, Ron often said, *"When you take the oath to defend the Constitution, that oath never expires."* Watching him live out those words made me—and many others—believe it.

Somewhere along the way, I received a small blue wrench beside my name in the chat —a sign that I had become a moderator for his livestream. It may sound simple, but that moment meant everything to me. It meant trust. And from then on, I was all in.

When *The People's Convoy* disbanded, Ron didn't stop. He remembered Senator Cruz's words: *"You need the people."* That became his next mission. Together with his **Wolf Pack**, he planned a cross-country walk to Washington, D.C.—to gather letters, meet Americans face-to-face, and carry their voices to the Capitol.

Those of us working behind the scenes handled logistics, media calls, law enforcement coordination, and community outreach. We were a team, united by purpose.

Halfway through the journey, in Illinois, Ron's shoulder pain grew unbearable. I helped find a doctor who confirmed what we feared—he needed surgery. We returned to Nevada, but the mission didn't end. Even during recovery, Ron stayed focused, researching, speaking out, and planning the next steps.

Through it all, he became more than a leader. He became family—a brother, a friend, a patriot who bleeds red, white, and blue. I once told him, *"Ron, I've got your back."* That promise still stands.

With love and respect,
Mama Wolf

On behalf of the **Wolf Pack**: Giovanna · Weather Cat · Texas Girl · Mr. T · Jen M. · Jennifer

ACKNOWLEDGMENTS

No book is ever written alone, and this one is no exception.

First, my deepest thanks to **the men and women of The People's Convoy**—drivers, supporters, and families—who proved that courage and unity still roll strong on America's highways. You reminded me that conviction and compassion can share the same road.

To my **Wolf Pack**—*Mama Wolf, Giovanna, Weather Cat, Texas Girl, Mr. T., Jen M* and *Jennifer*—thank you for your loyalty, strength, and tireless behind-the-scenes work. You carried the mission forward when the miles felt long.

To my **friends and followers online**, who tuned in, commented, encouraged, and prayed—you gave me reason to keep going, even when the road ahead was uncertain.

To the **veterans** who still live by the oath to defend the Constitution— you inspire me every day.

And finally, to my **family**—thank you for your patience, faith, and love. Every mile, every word, and every sleepless night spent chasing this dream was for you and for the country we all call home.

God bless America.

Author's Note

This book isn't about a convoy or a walk. Those were chapters in a larger story—the story of how an ordinary American decided to stand up, speak out, and help his country remember who she is.

Our founders designed a republic: a government run by the people, not a people run by the government. Over time, we drifted. Rules multiplied, trust thinned, and too many good folks began to feel like passengers in a nation they were meant to steer. My journey—on the road, in prayer, through blisters and miles—was never about politics. It was about responsibility. It was about keeping a promise to my neighbors, to my oath, and to the next generation.

I met thousands of Americans along the way: veterans who still salute, mothers who still pray, workers who still build, children who still believe. They didn't ask for perfection. They asked to be heard. I told them I would carry their voices forward. This book is part of keeping that promise.

If you take anything with you when you close these pages, let it be this: freedom isn't something we receive from Washington—it's something we guard together. Read, think, question, and stand—peacefully, firmly, with faith. The road back to the America our founders envisioned doesn't begin in a capital—it begins in the heart of every citizen who decides to act.

— Ron "Grey Wolf" Coleman

Table of Contents

FOREWORD..i

ACKNOWLEDGMENTS...ii

Author's Note iii

Chapter 1 – Where It All Began...1

Chapter 2 – The Awakening on the Road.....................................5

Chapter 3 – The Turning Point (2016-2019) 9

    The Road Starts to Move Again...9

    Conversations Across America...10

    The Noise Machine 10

    The Weight of Progress...11

    Signs in the Wind...11

    The Edge of the Storm 12

Chapter 4 – The Years of Fire (2020–2021) 13

    When the World Stopped 13

    The Mandate Machine 13

    The Summer of Fire 14

    The Election Storm...14

    The Engineer's Eye 15

    The Crackdown...15

    The Long Haul of Faith..16

    The Spark 16

Chapter 5 – The Breaking Point (2022) 19

    The Price of Control 19

    The Comfort That Cost Us Everything 20

    The Silencing 20

    The Breaking Point..21

    Preparation...22

    The Drive to Adelanto...22

    Arrival in Adelanto...23

Chapter 6 – The Convoy Begins...25

Chapter 7 – Rolling East..31

Chapter 8 – Waking the Nation 37

Chapter 9 – Oklahoma Rising (The Road to Elk City).........43

Chapter 10 – The Eagle Over Big Cabin...................................49

Chapter 11 – The Road to Cuba (Day Seven) 53

Chapter 12 – The Flag...59

Chapter 13 – The Layover in Monrovia 65

   The Night of the Flag 65

   The Day of Rest 67

   The Grandfather and the Pocket Constitutions 67

   The Evening Rally 68

Chapter 14 – Just One Day Away 71

Chapter 15 – Just One More Push (The Road to Hagerstown) 75

Chapter 16 – Seventy Miles to Washington 81

Chapter 17 – Carrying the People's Voice 87

Chapter 18 – The Road Beyond the Capitol 93

   The Echo After the Applause 93

   A Visit from Senator Cruz 93

   The Fracture in the Ranks 95

   From Driver to Teacher 96

   A Movement in the Making 98

   Back on the Road 98

   The Quiet Realization 99

   The Teacher Becomes the Walker 99

   The Next Call to the Road 100

Chapter 19 – The Call to Walk 103

   Back Behind the Wheel 103

   The First Sketches of a Walk 104

   The Road Home 104

   Preparation in Reno 105

   A Sudden Loss 105

   The Arrival of Mr. T 106

Chapter 20 – The Night Before the Walk 107

   Reflections and Resolve 107

   Final Preparations 108

   The Quiet Before Dawn 109

Chapter 21 – The First Steps 111

   No Crowd, No Fanfare 111

   The Flag and the Faith 112

   Sunday Morning 113

   Stagecoach and the Symbols 113

   The Fourth of July 114

   The Mustangs 115

Chapter 22 – The Weight and the Worth 117

   The Fifty Horse Ranch 118

Over the Hill and Into Purpose 119

Fallon and the Healing 120

Chapter 23 – Lessons from the Road..............................*123*

The Road Calls Again...123

Salt Wells..124

Return to Fallon 125

Visitors and Volunteers...126

The Preamble in the Desert 127

Encounters on the Highway 128

Sand Mountain...128

Chapter 24 – The Climb and the Healing *131*

Chapter 25 – Bubba's Return and New Roads *137*

The Return to the Hundred-Mile Marker 138

The Walk Back to Middlegate 140

Cold Springs Station 141

Chapter 26 – Cold Springs Station (The Brotherhood Forms) *145*

Chapter 27 – The Gathering (A Convoy of Patriots) *151*

The Third Morning 152

Across New Pass..153

The Arrival 155

The Morning of the Hat 155

The Road to Austin 157

Chapter 28 – The Trial in Austin *159*

Chapter 29 — The Road Reawakens.............................*167*

Beechy Is Peachy — August 10, 2022 168

Good Vibrations — August 11 169

Chapter 30 — The Turning Point *171*

Chapter 31 – The Iron Road *177*

Chapter 32 – The Silent Fair...*181*

Chapter 33 – Come Talk About Freedom *185*

Chapter 34 – Different Flags, Same Fight......................*189*

Chapter 35 – Spanish Fork (A Stirring in the Spirit) *195*

Chapter 36 – Fading Echoes...*203*

Chapter 37 – The Long Plain...*213*

Chapter 38 – The Messenger's Weight *219*

Chapter 39 – The Long Road to Hannibal......................*223*

Chapter 40 – The Weight of the Republic *229*

Chapter 41 – The Long Road Home *235*

Epilogue...243
Thanks..244
About the Author...245

Chapter 1 – Where It All Began

The hum of my Kenworth's diesel engine was steady that day, a low growl beneath the static of the CB and the satellite radio. Somewhere along a stretch of interstate between loads, I pulled into a truck-stop café for dinner. On the TV above the counter, a man was descending a golden escalator in New York City—*Donald J. Trump, announcing he was running for President of the United States.*

At first, I barely looked up. Another rich man chasing headlines, I thought. I'd seen plenty of promises come and go in my lifetime. But there was something about that image—the gleam of gold, the confidence in his voice—that stayed with me long after I climbed back into my truck. Maybe it was the way he talked straight, maybe the way the crowd reacted, but I felt something I hadn't felt in a long time: curiosity—maybe even a *spark of hope.*

By then I'd spent most of my life on the road. My story started in Reno, Nevada, back when the town still felt small. My father worked hard, my mother kept the family centered, and Sunday mornings meant church—Baptist on his side, Catholic on hers. They met somewhere in the middle, and I was raised Catholic, going to catechism and a parochial school where the nuns could set you straight with a single look.

Faith, family, and work were the rules of our house. You respected your elders, stood for the flag, and never took more than you earned. I remember my first Black classmate in fourth grade—a quiet kid who became my friend by the end of the week. To us, the world was simple: play ball, do your homework, treat people right.

Some memories never fade. I can still see myself sitting in the back seat of my father's car in November 1963, waiting at a red light near the hospital where my mother was being released after giving birth to my brother. The radio crackled with the news that President John F. Kennedy had been shot. My father's knuckles went white on the steering wheel, and tears welled in his eyes. It was the first time I'd ever seen him cry. *Even as a boy, I knew something had changed.*

As the world moved through the sixties, seventies, and eighties, America changed too—wars overseas, protests at home, and scandals in

Washington. Each one left a generation wondering what had happened to the country our parents believed in. When my turn came, I joined the United States Air Force.

The Air Force taught me discipline, patience, and pride in serving something larger than myself. The day I raised my right hand and swore to protect and defend the Constitution, those words burned into me. That oath doesn't expire when the uniform comes off—it becomes part of who you are.

During those years I met people from every background and faith. On weekends I'd sometimes sit in on different services—Baptist, Jewish, Buddhist—trying to understand what faith meant to others. It reminded me that America's strength was its freedom to believe, or not believe, without fear.

When I left the Air Force, I wanted to stay close to the sky. I'd spent years as a KC-135 crew chief and knew my way around every Boeing that flew, but the airlines weren't hiring. Back then people joked that someone had to die for a new job to open. I took whatever honest work I could find—from turning wrenches in wrecking yards to managing a McDonald's for a spell—anything to keep moving forward.

In 1981, I stumbled into a new world: telecommunications. The breakup of AT&T had created opportunities in "alternative long-distance," and I hired on as an operations technician. Over the next two decades I climbed through the ranks, learning satellite and microwave-radio systems, traveling the world, and eventually serving as a vice president of operations and engineering. I saw technology shrink the planet and connect people in ways my younger self could never have imagined.

By 2003 I was ready for a change. I left corporate life, bought an auto-repair shop near Salinas, California, and spent six good years there before selling the business and returning home to Nevada. That's when the open road called again. Driving a truck felt like coming full circle—still working with machines, still solving problems, still chasing the horizon.

The cab became my classroom. I tuned the radio from talk shows to C-SPAN, listening to the noise of politics and wondering when common sense had left the room. Every new regulation seemed to come from someone who'd never built anything or spent a day behind the wheel. Out on the road I met other drivers who felt the same—that the harder we worked, the tighter things got.

Sometimes, late at night, I'd pull into a rest area, kill the engine, and let the silence settle. That's when the questions hit hardest. How did a nation built on independence end up drowning in red tape? Why were honest folks always the ones paying for mistakes made in high offices?

When Trump came down that escalator, those questions didn't disappear—but suddenly they felt like they might have answers. He wasn't a career politician, and that alone caught my attention. I didn't know yet if he could deliver, but he was challenging a system that needed it. For a man like me—veteran, small-business owner, trucker—that meant something.

That day in the truck stop marked the start of *my own awakening*. From then on, I paid closer attention, read more history, and started to believe that maybe the American spirit wasn't gone after all—it was just waiting for someone to remind us what it looked like.

Chapter 2 – The Awakening on the Road

Long before podcasts filled every cab and commute, my education came through static and diesel hum. I listened to how people in power talked about the same country I drove across every day. Some nights, after a thousand miles of asphalt, I wondered if anyone in Washington had ever set foot on the ground I was covering. It didn't feel like it.

Out there, patterns appear that city folks miss. I saw factories gone dark, small towns where For Sale signs outnumbered mailboxes, and storefronts that never reopened after the last recession. But I also saw pride that refused to die—flags still flying, churches still open, families still holding on.

Those miles taught me something important: America wasn't broken. It was just being ignored.

At truck stops I'd talk with other drivers over sometimes bad coffee and better stories. We all felt the same frustration—the rules kept multiplying, the taxes kept climbing, and the people writing those rules didn't seem to understand what a fourteen-hour day behind the wheel actually felt like. Most of the folks making decisions had never been behind the wheel of a semi-truck rolling down the highway, never built anything with their hands, never watched a sunset from the shoulder of I-80 with diesel on their breath.

That's when I started digging deeper—reading the Constitution, studying how government was meant to work. Somewhere between the on-ramps and rest areas, I began to see how power gathers, how money moves, and how easily independence slips away when people stop paying attention.

I learned that before 1913, America didn't even have a federal income tax. The country ran mostly on tariffs—on what we made and shipped to the world. Other nations wanted what America built, and the money from those exports built our roads and schools.

That all changed after 1913, when Washington created the income tax and the Federal Reserve. They said it was temporary, a wartime necessity—but government never lets go once it takes hold. What started as a stopgap became a permanent weight on the working man's back.

One night in Commerce City, Colorado, I found myself arguing politics with a handful of drivers. One said, "I don't get how Trump thinks he's gonna bring manufacturing back. It's gone."

I told him, *"Let's say I'm President Trump. I sit down with a car company that moved its factory to Mexico. I say, 'How about bringing that plant home?' They say, 'No way—labor's cheap down there, and we're staying put.' So I offer incentives —subsidies, tax credits, help building a new plant. Still no. Then I say, 'All right. For every car you sell in the United States that wasn't built here, we'll slap a 35-percent tariff on it.' Now the math changes."*

He stared for a second, then nodded. "Never thought of it like that."

That was the thing—I wasn't just listening to politics anymore; I was learning what it meant for people like us. The more I studied our history —the Revolution, the Civil War, the rise and fall of industries—the more I understood what had been lost.

The 2016 campaign rolled across my radio dial like a constant storm. I listened to both sides—Republicans and Democrats alike—but most of what I heard from career politicians was noise: rehearsed lines, recycled promises.

Trump was different. Not careful, not polished—but direct. When he spoke about bringing manufacturing back and putting American workers first, it hit home. I'd seen too many towns hollowed out to ignore that message.

At another diner in Missouri, I found myself debating tariffs again with a driver who worried prices would soar. I told him I believed tariffs could actually bring industries back home—many of them American companies to begin with. There might be some short-term pain, I said, but in the long run, it would mean lasting strength and opportunity. We talked it through and realized we both wanted the same thing—a fair shot for American workers.

During those years, I kept a small voice recorder on the dash, filling it with notes and questions. Why did everything cost more when we were told the economy was booming? Why were regulations written by people who'd never touched a wrench? Why did working harder seem to count for less every year?

Somewhere between the miles, the answers began to take shape. It wasn't about a single man—it was about a message. For people like me, who'd spent decades feeling invisible, it felt like the country had finally heard us knocking.

Out there in the glow of the dashboard lights, I thought back on all those miles and all those nights of wondering. For the first time in a long time, I believed that maybe—just maybe—the American story wasn't over yet.

Chapter 3 – The Turning Point (2016-2019)

Election Night 2016 is burned into my memory.

I was parked at a truck stop in Las Vegas, three televisions hanging above the counter, each blaring the same anxious commentary. Maps of red and blue flashed across the screens, pundits stumbling over their own predictions as the unthinkable started to unfold. Around me, forks stopped clinking against plates. Coffee went cold in cups. The room fell into a hush that felt almost sacred.

When the final numbers rolled in and it became clear that **Donald Trump** had won, half the room erupted in disbelief, half in cautious cheers. I didn't shout or celebrate. I just sat there, staring at the map, thinking how—for the first time in a long time—it felt like America had grabbed the wheel again. Not the politicians, not the lobbyists, but the people.

That night changed something in me.

It wasn't just about an election; it was about momentum. You could feel it in the air the next morning, like the first rumble of a diesel after a long winter—raw, powerful, alive.

***

The Road Starts to Move Again

In the weeks that followed, conversations at truck stops shifted. The usual talk about weather fronts and freight rates turned to politics. Drivers who'd never cared one way or the other suddenly had opinions. "You think he'll really do it?" someone asked over the CB near Amarillo.
"Bring the jobs back?"
Nobody knew. But the question itself—the hope behind it—felt new.

As I rolled east through Missouri and into Tennessee, I started to notice the difference firsthand. Warehouses that had sat half-empty for years now had lights on at night. Dispatchers sounded busier, less beaten down. Freight was up, and fuel prices were steady enough that a man could plan a week without wondering if he'd still make rent.

You could feel the hum of something rebuilding.

The media didn't see it that way. Every headline screamed crisis, every anchor warned division. But out here on the road, I saw the opposite—neighbors fixing fences together, small shops reopening, American flags reappearing on porches that hadn't seen one since 9/11. It wasn't arrogance; it was pride. Quiet, working-class pride.

***

Conversations Across America

In diners from Ohio to Oklahoma, the talk was the same: things feel different. Some folks were skeptical, others hopeful, but most just wanted the country to work again. I remember fueling outside Joplin when a young clerk behind the counter said, "Guess people are spending again. Maybe things are turning around." He said it like a man who'd been waiting to believe in something.

At another diner in Missouri, I ended up in a debate about tariffs with a driver who swore prices would skyrocket. I told him what I believed—that a short-term pinch could mean long-term gain if it brought manufacturing back home. "It's not punishment," I said. "It's correction." By the end of the meal, we both realized we wanted the same thing: a fair shot for American workers.

Moments like that reminded me how much common ground still existed once the noise was stripped away.

***

The Noise Machine

But the noise never stopped. Back in Washington, it was Russia this, impeachment that—day after day of outrage meant to keep people angry and distracted. Out here, the only collusion we cared about was between bad weather and tight deadlines. We just kept hauling.

By 2018, business was booming. Loads were steady, paychecks stronger, and optimism was spreading like good news used to. Yet if you turned on the TV, you'd think the country was burning down. That disconnect ate at me. The America I saw through my windshield didn't match the America on the screen.

That's when I stopped trusting commentary and started trusting my own eyes.

I began keeping notes—little observations scribbled on fuel receipts and logbook margins. The waitress in Ohio whose husband finally got a raise. The mechanic in Georgia training two new apprentices. The driver in Texas who said, "Feels like we matter again." They weren't statistics; they were the pulse of a nation that was waking up.

***

The Weight of Progress

Still, progress always draws resistance.
For every job site that came back to life, a pundit warned collapse. For every new factory, a bureaucrat demanded another regulation. It was like watching someone try to kill momentum with paperwork. And somewhere behind it all, I could sense the machinery of politics grinding its gears—those who thrived on division trying to jam the engine just as it was catching speed.

From the driver's seat of a Kenworth, you get used to reading the road. You can tell when a storm's building long before the sky turns. That's what those years felt like: air thick with static, something forming on the horizon.

***

Signs in the Wind

By 2019, that uneasy hum had turned into a vibration you could feel in your chest. People talked sharper, argued quicker. Old friends at truck stops skipped certain topics altogether. It wasn't just politics; it was fatigue—the kind that seeps into a nation's bones.

I'd listen to the satellite radio during long hauls—one channel praising progress, the next predicting collapse. Both missed the truth I was living daily: America was still working, still moving, but cracks were spreading beneath the asphalt. You could sense a pushback growing against everything that had been rebuilt.

Then came the whispers: a virus overseas, something spreading fast in China. Most of us laughed it off. We'd seen scares before—bird flu, swine flu, SARS. The world always kept spinning. But this time felt different, even if I couldn't yet say why.

***

The Edge of the Storm

That winter, I rolled west through Kansas under a sky the color of steel. My gut told me change was coming—the kind that doesn't ask permission. The headlines were getting stranger, the tone darker. Somewhere between dispatch calls and weather reports, the word lockdown started to appear. Nobody knew what it meant yet.

Out on the interstate, America still looked the same—diesels roaring, diners open, flags flying—but something invisible was already moving through the air. I remember glancing at my reflection in the side mirror and wondering, How far will they take this? How much are we willing to give up?

I didn't know it then, but that question would define the next three years of my life—and ultimately, the journey that would become the *Grey Wolf Walk Across America for Freedom.*

The tremors were there. The fault line was already forming. All that was left was for the ground to break.

Chapter 4 – The Years of Fire (2020–2021)

The years 2020 and 2021 cut through American life like a fault line—splitting everything we thought we knew about freedom, truth, and trust. Looking back, they weren't just chaotic years; they were testing years. Years that burned away illusion and showed us what we were really made of.

***

When the World Stopped

I was hauling a return load west from the East Coast when the first serious reports hit the radio. "Wuhan." "Lockdowns." "Outbreak." Within weeks, those words turned from background noise into marching orders. Fifteen days to slow the spread became school closures, shuttered churches, and empty streets.

Nevada went dark.

Casinos that had never closed—not for fires, floods, or holidays—locked their doors. Even the slot machines in corner stores went black. Truck-stop diners taped cardboard signs across their doors: **NO ENTRY – COVID RESTRICTIONS.**

I'd just hauled critical supplies halfway across the country, but I couldn't buy a cup of coffee inside. They called us essential but treated us like something stinky on the bottom of their shoes.

So we adapted—coolers instead of diners, sandwiches instead of hot meals. We kept rolling. That's what truckers do. It wasn't the first time we'd carried the country on our backs, but it was the first time we'd done it while being locked out of the very world we were keeping alive.

***

The Mandate Machine

At first it was fear. Then it became control.

Orders rolled out faster than we could read them—masks, curfews, "essential" and "non-essential" labels. Bureaucrats stood behind podiums on television telling Americans how to live, while families fell apart under the weight of isolation.

Then came the vaccine mandates. What had been promised as the ticket back to normal became the price of admission to society. When companies began threatening jobs over a shot, I knew a line had been crossed.

"Mandates aren't laws," I told people. "They're orders dressed up to look official."

But fear shouted louder than reason.

***

The Summer of Fire

Then the streets ignited.

I rolled through one Midwest city after another, passing boarded-up windows and burned patrol cars while the news called it "mostly peaceful." Families swept ash from their doorways as politicians argued semantics. In the same breath, those same leaders demanded *Defund the Police*.

The same officers who'd been heroes weeks earlier were now villains. It broke my heart. Even the games that once brought us together had become battlegrounds—players kneeling while the anthem played. That flag wasn't a prop—it was a promise.

By then I knew this wasn't just politics. It was spiritual. America's moral compass was spinning, and too many seemed content to drift wherever it pointed.

***

The Election Storm

As 2020 staggered toward November, the whole country trembled with tension. Governors and courts rewrote election rules on the fly— mail-in ballots, drop boxes, last-minute counting extensions. The airwaves buzzed with "historic" and "unprecedented."

I parked at a rest area in Kansas on election night, tablet propped on the dash, watching numbers flash like slot machines. Votes don't vanish mid-count—but that night, they did. Tallies dropped on one side and rose on the other by the same amount. Maybe it was glitches. Maybe not. Either way, the trust that bound Americans together snapped.

When the dust settled, anger wasn't the strongest feeling—betrayal was. Something between citizen and state had broken.

***

The Engineer's Eye

Before I came back to trucking full-time, I'd spent over twenty years in communications and engineering—helping build the backbone of global networks. I worked in fiber optics, satellites, and microwave systems, designing connections that carried voices and data around the world. In that world, precision and integrity weren't options—they were survival.

So when I began digging into how our election systems actually functioned, I couldn't help viewing it through an engineer's lens. Those voting machines ran on ordinary Windows operating systems using SQL databases—editable, network-capable, anything but immutable. Secure systems don't work that way. They rely on blockchain-like, write-once architecture.

What I saw wasn't a conspiracy theory—it was bad engineering, and bad engineering leaves doors open. Whether those doors were used or not, no honest system should have them.

That realization hit me harder than any headline. The more I looked, the clearer it became: this wasn't chaos by accident. Somewhere, someone wanted confusion.

***

The Crackdown

January 6th hit like a thunderclap.

Millions had gathered in Washington to protest peacefully, but before the first bus even reached the capital, the story was written:

Insurrection.

By nightfall, every voice that questioned anything—from election procedures to lockdowns—was branded dangerous. Social media platforms turned into firing lines. I lost three YouTube channels and three Twitter accounts—not for hate, not for violence, but for asking questions.

It wasn't freedom of speech anymore; it was permission-based speech.

I'd grown up believing the First Amendment was sacred. Now it felt conditional.

***

The Long Haul of Faith

Through it all, the road stayed honest. Asphalt doesn't lie; it just demands you stay awake. Each mile gave me time to think about what was happening to my country.

Fear had turned into habit. People accepted things they never would have accepted just a few years earlier—checkpoints, mask patrols, digital passes. You could watch freedom being redefined in real time, and most folks were too tired to fight it.

But beneath that fatigue, something was stirring. Americans can bend, but we don't stay bent for long.

Resolve. That's what I began to feel in the wind again.

***

The Spark

Then came the sound that reignited everything—the horns of Canadian truckers rolling across frozen highways. Their convoy protesting government mandates wasn't just noise; it was a wake-up call.

I watched from my living-room screen in Nevada, goosebumps rising as those rigs thundered through snow and sleet, flags snapping in the wind. The courage was contagious.

Messages started lighting up driver groups and CB channels— rumors of an American convoy forming.
The moment I heard it, I knew: I wasn't done. None of us were.

All the frustration, the sleepless miles, the conversations in diners and parking lots—it had all been leading here.

This wasn't about politics anymore; it was about people standing up again.

That night, after shutting down my rig, I sat in the bunk staring at the small flag hanging in my sleeper. The road outside was dark, but something inside me burned bright again.

It was time to carry that flag farther than I ever had before.

It was time to roll.

Chapter 5 – The Breaking Point (2022)

January 2022 didn't feel like a new year. It felt like a reckoning.

The echoes of those Canadian horns still rang in my mind, but now the question wasn't *who will stand?*—it was *when do we leave?*

Two years of fear, mandates, and division had left America bruised and exhausted. The air on the road felt heavier somehow, as if the whole nation was holding its breath. Folks no longer trusted the headlines—or the people writing them. They trusted what they could see with their own eyes, and what most of us saw wasn't recovery. It was erosion.

At truck stops and diners—where we were still allowed inside—the talk had changed. No one was arguing about freight rates or football scores anymore. It was about truth, censorship, and survival. Over coffee, the same question kept surfacing:

What happened to us? When did freedom become conditional?

I'd heard those questions echo from coast to coast since 2020, but by '22, something was different. The fear was wearing thin, replaced by resolve. America had been locked down, shamed, and silenced. Now people were simply done.

***

The Price of Control

The government called them stimulus checks. I called them payoffs.

Twelve hundred dollars at a time, they bought compliance under the banner of compassion. "Here's your help," they said. "Now stay home. Don't ask questions."

Then came the extended unemployment benefits. They called it relief, but it was really sedation — a way to dull the pain while the economy was carved up. For the first time in my life, I saw help do more harm than hardship.

A manager in a Troutdale truck stop restaurant told me, "I can't get people back. Why would anyone flip burgers for twelve bucks and hour when the government pays an equivalent of eighteen to stay home?"

He was right. Work had always been the backbone of this country — not just for a paycheck, but for pride. Take away purpose, and a man starts to forget who he is. When people stop working, they stop dreaming. When they stop dreaming, they stop defending the ground beneath their feet.

It wasn't compassion that drove those policies — it was control. The kind that doesn't march in boots, but slides quietly through screens and direct deposits.

***

The Comfort That Cost Us Everything

The world adjusted — delivery groceries, remote jobs, virtual classrooms. It looked efficient, even impressive. But I could feel the poison in it.

When life gets too easy, people stop questioning why. Convenience kills curiosity. Comfort without purpose breeds apathy.

We learned to live behind screens. Families sat in the same house and barely spoke. Churches were dark while casinos blazed in neon. Liquor stores were essential, but prayer wasn't.

I hauled freight through towns where people still wore masks walking alone. Fear had outlasted logic and common sense. It wasn't about health anymore; it was about obedience.

The message was clear: sit down, stay quiet, and be grateful for what you're given.

But freedom doesn't survive on gratitude — it survives on grit.

***

The Silencing

By mid-2021, fear had hardened into something worse — fatigue. "Fifteen days to slow the spread" had become two years of shifting rules and endless contradictions.
The phrase trust the science had turned into don't ask questions.

By then I'd already lost those YouTube channels and Twitter accounts — erased for saying what half the country was thinking. I wasn't spreading hate. I was spreading doubt — and doubt had become forbidden.

Freedom of speech had turned into permission-based speech. The kind you had to earn by agreeing with the herd.

But under that blanket of silence, something else began to grow — a quiet, steady determination. You can't kill truth with censorship; you only prove it's dangerous.

I could hear it even through the static of the CB radio. Drivers who'd once argued over freight rates were now quoting the Constitution. They were angry, but not reckless — angry in the way a soldier gets before he stands his post.

***

The Breaking Point

By late January, it was all I could think about. Dispatch chatter buzzed with rumors. Facebook groups sprang up overnight. Truckers, veterans, farmers — different people, same purpose.

I knew I had to go.

That night I sat in the cab, dash lights glowing like coals in the dark, the logbook open but empty. I thought about my father — a man who worked until his hands cracked and bled, a man who believed that freedom wasn't inherited, it was earned.

He would have hated what America had become — a nation bribed into silence.

I thought about the oath I took in the Air Force:

"To protect and defend the Constitution of the United States against all enemies, foreign and domestic."

That oath doesn't expire.

It doesn't wear out. It just waits — until the day you have to live it again.

I closed the logbook and said aloud, *"It's time."*

***

Preparation

The next morning, the desert sky was pale and cold when I stepped outside. My 1991 Kenworth sat in the driveway like an old warhorse waiting for orders, her chrome catching the first faint shimmer of dawn. The air was still, expectant, like the quiet before a long haul.

I'd dropped the trailer, mounted the heavy tow attachment, and began my ritual: checking tire pressure, oil, belts, and brake lines. It was more than maintenance—it was meditation.

Neighbors waved as we exchanged glances across the yards, probably thinking I was gearing up for another long run. I didn't bother correcting them. This trip wasn't about freight. It was about freedom.

Inside the cab, I packed the essentials—maps, tools, a cooler full of sandwiches, and the flag that had ridden with me for what felt like a lifetime.

As I tightened the chains and binders on the tow unit, a thought returned—the same one that had followed me for months: *If not us, who? If not now, when?*

***

The Drive to Adelanto

I left Reno before noon, heading south on Highway 395. The city fell away behind me, the Sierras standing tall and silent against a pale winter sky. Carson City slid past, then Minden—familiar names, each mile carrying me farther from comfort and closer to conviction.

The road wound along Topaz Lake, its surface rimmed with ice, before climbing toward Mammoth Lakes. Snow began to fall on the pass, heavy and wet—the kind that makes every turn feel like a question. The wipers beat a steady rhythm as the old Kenworth dug in, engine growling low against the grade.

By the time I cleared the summit, the world had turned silver—snow on the peaks, sun on the valley floor. Lone Pine came and went, and then the desert opened wide. The highway stretched south like a promise, unbroken and endless.

The CB was mostly quiet except for the hum of passing rigs. Somewhere near Olancha, a voice broke through the static.
"You headed south, driver?"
"Adelanto," I answered.
There was a pause. Then: "Godspeed, brother."

Those two words said everything.

The miles rolled by—ridge after ridge, sky, sand and silence. Out there, the desert tells the truth. There's nowhere to hide from it.

As the sun sank behind the mountains, I thought about everything that had brought me here—the lockdowns, the fear, the way neighbors had turned wary of one another. And I thought about how quickly a country can lose its footing when its people forget their own power.

Freedom isn't a product of government. It's a practice of the heart.

***

Arrival in Adelanto

By the time I rolled into Adelanto that Monday night, February 21st, the desert was wrapped in darkness and cold. I was the second truck to arrive. The lot beside the stadium was quiet—just a few cars idling under the sodium lights, their exhaust drifting like ghostly banners in the night.

A driver with a flatbed was working to mount a forty-foot banner across his trailer. I pulled up facing him, flipped on my high beams and spotlights to give him light, and helped where I could—steadying rope, tightening bungees, securing corners against the wind. We didn't talk much; we didn't have to. The work spoke for us.

When the sign was finally stretched tight, we stepped back to look at it—forty feet of vinyl spelling out the words we all felt in our bones. He clapped me on the shoulder. "Looks like we're making history, brother."

A few more people trickled in as the night wore on—mostly truckers, a handful of RVs, a couple of families bringing supplies. Someone invited me into their coach for hot dogs, coffee and conversation. We sat around the table swapping stories—about the road, about freedom, about why we'd come. It felt like family forming right there in the desert.

When I finally climbed back into my cab, the lot was still and quiet again. I thought of all the people still out there, making their way here.

Tomorrow, I knew, this place would come alive.

Chapter 6 – The Convoy Begins

At sunrise, I woke to a different world. The lot had indeed come alive—trucks, cars, RVs, and well-wishers everywhere. When I opened the door to climb out after getting some rest in my sleeper, I found three brown paper bags sitting on my steps. Inside were fruit, chips, cookies, a few dollars, and handwritten notes thanking the truckers for standing up for freedom and liberty.

A little later that morning, the press began to arrive—independent reporters and the mainstream alike—asking why we were there, what we hoped to accomplish. I gave a few interviews, trying to put into words what so many of us felt: that this was about more than mandates. It was about reclaiming our voice.

Supporters came bearing gifts—food, water, blankets—and stories. They shook hands, hugged, and cried. One young girl, maybe three or four years old, ran up and wrapped her arms around my leg. She looked up and said softly, "Thank you."

Her mother stood nearby holding a big drawing—maybe two feet square—that the little girl had made herself. It showed a truck with an American flag over the front, a truck with a Canadian flag over the front, a heart with "Woooo" inside of it, and a simple message in crayon: *"Let's Go Trucker's—Freedom—I* ♡ *Trucker's,"* signed *"Chloe."*

That moment hit me hard. It reminded me why I was there—not just for myself, but for that little girl, for her family, for everyone who still believed freedom was worth standing for.

The People's Convoy was about to roll, and deep down, I knew—this was the beginning of something bigger than any of us.

After that moment with Chloe and her mom, more and more people started coming up—people who just wanted to see us off, handing us money, hugging us, and telling their stories of why they were there. Then came more media, trying to find out what we hoped to accomplish with our drive across the country.

I remember telling reporters that for me, it wasn't just about mandates for masks or vaccines tied to keeping a job—it was about

Drawing by Chloe, Adelanto, CA. — February 2022

freedom itself. We wanted to remind everyone we met not to comply blindly, but to think, to research, and to question before surrendering their God given rights.

Some reporters looked at me in disbelief. One asked, "Well, how are you going to survive? How will you pay your bills if you're not working?" I told them straight, "If it means I become homeless and have to sleep in my truck—so be it. My truck is my home, and the word must get out."

Donations were pouring in. A few of the trucks that had shown up on the 22nd began loading their empty 53-foot vans with supplies that people had been bringing in for the last couple of days—cases of water, chips, toiletries, blankets, jackets—you name it. Because this wasn't just a convoy of semi-trucks. It was a convoy of everything: semis, pickups, cars, vans, RVs, campers, even a motorcycle or two.

That evening, I went back to the same coach I'd visited the night I arrived and met a couple of doctors who were friends with the owner— **Dr. Paul Alexander** and **Dr. Pierre Kory**. Dr. Alexander was doing a live podcast at the time and began asking questions about what was happening there in Adelanto. Since I was one of the drivers, he asked if I'd be willing to do an interview. I agreed, not realizing then how much they would enjoy our conversation. That short interview turned into the start of a real friendship between the three of us.

Later that night, on the 22nd, I crawled into my sleeper and fell asleep with the hum of distant voices still echoing outside. Early the next morning—the 23rd—I woke before sunrise to the sound of engines, laughter, and excitement. When I opened my door again, there were more brown paper bags stacked on my steps. I'd lost count. I started tucking them up on my upper bunk in the sleeper—each one filled with snacks, notes, and love from people who believed in what we were doing.

More parents with children came up to shake hands, more hugs, more tears. People told us they wished they could come along. Drivers began meeting for coordination sessions, listening to updates from the convoy organizers. The air buzzed with energy and purpose.

Soon, we'd be rolling out of Adelanto—and the movement would be underway

After mounting two flagpoles on the back of my truck—three flags flying proud: Old Glory at the top center, the POW/MIA below it, and the "Don't Tread on Me" on the driver's-side pole—I lined up with the convoy after our driver's meeting. I was second in line to roll out.

Just before we rolled out, a reporter from One America News Network—**Stefan Kleinhenz**—approached me and asked if he could ride along to Arizona for the first leg of the convoy. I told him, *"Sure."* Having a reporter embedded in my truck for that first stretch felt like a good way to show the world what this was really about.

Then came the call over the CB: the California Highway Patrol would be assisting us onto Highway 58 from Highway 395, then again through Barstow and onto Interstate 15 before merging east onto I-40 toward Arizona.

As we rolled out of Adelanto and onto 395, we made a short stop just north of the lot we started in. In my rearview mirrors, I could see a sea of American flags waving from cars, trucks, and RVs. People lined both sides of the road, cheering, shouting "Freedom!" and blowing kisses as we passed. The air was thick with pride and emotion.

As we continued north on 395 and merged onto Highway 58, the California Highway Patrol was waiting to escort us for a stretch. Officers parked on the shoulders some of them sticking their arms out the windows, giving us a thumbs-up as we passed. We rolled east toward Barstow, then onto I-15 and I-40. Every overpass along the way was packed—families, veterans, and supporters waving flags and holding homemade signs.

We blew our horns in response to the cheers and raised fists from the bridges. By the time we reached Needles, California, the sight ahead stopped us cold. The local fire department had parked its ladder truck on top of the overpass, the ladder extended high with a massive American flag waving proudly in the desert wind. On either side stood more fire trucks and ambulances, their lights flashing red and blue against the afternoon sun, sirens blaring in salute. Hundreds of people crowded the bridge and lined the road below, waving, cheering, and holding their flags high as we rolled beneath them.

Overpass in Needles, CA. Day one of The Peoples Convoy — February 2022

As we crossed into Arizona, the show of support only grew stronger. Every overpass seemed to be alive with color—red, white, and blue everywhere you looked. It wasn't just a convoy rolling down the highway; it was a living, breathing reminder that the American spirit was still alive and unbroken.

By the time we pulled into Golden Valley that evening, night had settled over the desert, on the drive in from I-40, I'd watched the sun sink behind the jagged hills, painting the sky in streaks of orange and gold.

The owner of a local pizza place had opened his parking lot to us, and as we parked our rigs, the warm smell of food filled the air. Inside, tables overflowed with pizza, brisket, and cold drinks—free for every driver, volunteer, and friend who rolled in that night.

We were tired, dusty, and hungry, but the energy in that parking lot was electric. Strangers laughed together, shared stories, and hugged like old friends. It was more than a meal—it was community. And as I looked around at the faces lit by the glow of headlights and neon signs, I realized something important: this wasn't just a convoy anymore. It was a movement—a rolling declaration that freedom still mattered.

It was a sight to behold—people united not by politics or party, but by a shared belief that freedom was worth standing up for. That first night set the tone for everything that was to come.

Inside, the atmosphere was alive. Drivers, volunteers, and locals crowded together, shaking hands and swapping stories over paper plates and steaming pizza. The smell of barbecue hung thick in the air, mingling with the laughter and hum of diesel engines cooling outside. Strangers became friends in minutes, united by the same purpose and the same word that had brought us all here—freedom. Someone cranked up a country song on a portable speaker, and for a few hours, the weight of the world seemed lighter. I remember stepping outside, looking across the line of idling trucks lit by amber running lights, and thinking:

This is what America looks like when it remembers who it is.

Chapter 7 – Rolling East

When I woke the next morning in Golden Valley, the first thing I smelled was coffee. Someone said the pizza place had opened early to serve breakfast, so I climbed out of my sleeper, crossed the dirt parking lot, and stepped inside. The same waitresses and workers who'd stayed late the night before were already there again—hair tied back, aprons dusted with flour, frying eggs, sausage, and potatoes while the scent of coffee filled the room.

I grabbed a paper plate, filled it with scrambled eggs, potatoes, and a couple of sausage links, and found a spot at one of the crowded tables. The chatter rolled like an engine idling—drivers swapping stories, locals thanking us, everyone talking about where the convoy was headed next. Someone at my table said it felt like history in the making. Another joked that we were all "truckers turned patriots overnight." We laughed, but everyone knew there was truth in it.

What felt like a few minutes turned into almost an hour, and when I finally looked up, the line of people was out the door. I gave up my seat so someone else could eat and stepped outside into the crisp desert air.

That's when I saw her—a familiar face that made me do a double take.

"I know you," I said.

It was **Sara Carter**, the journalist. She smiled and asked if I'd be willing to do an interview after she grabbed a cup of coffee. I gave her my phone number and started walking back toward my truck. As I made my way around the dirt lot, chatting with a few others doing the same, I saw Sara a few yards away.

A moment later, my phone rang.

"Where are you?" she asked. "Right behind you," I said with a laugh.

She turned around and laughed too—standing there with a cameraman and a sound tech. Sara was friendly, focused, all business wrapped in warmth. She interviewed me right there in the lot for a segment scheduled to air that evening on *Hannity*. She asked what this convoy was really about, and I told her straight: it wasn't about masks or mandates anymore—it was about freedom, and about reminding our country that the people still had a voice.

She nodded as I spoke, eyes intent. When she finished, she asked if I knew anyone else who might be willing to talk. I pointed out a few drivers who'd been there from the beginning, and soon enough she was interviewing them too, capturing their stories and hopes for the road ahead. For a few hours, it felt like the world was listening.

But as we rolled east later that day, news came crackling over the radio and phones alike—Russia had invaded Ukraine. In an instant, every headline shifted, every network pivoted. *Hannity's* schedule changed, and the interviews from Golden Valley never aired. That was the moment I realized how quickly truth can get buried when the world decides to look the other way.

A little later, the organizers gathered everyone near the front of the lot. The lead truck's flatbed had been turned into a makeshift stage, and **Brian Brase** climbed up with a microphone in hand. The chatter quieted. "Let's start this day right," he said.

We began with the **Pledge of Allegiance**. Hundreds of hands went to hearts. Eyes focused on the flag on the pole. Voices rose together, echoing between rows of trucks and RVs. When the last words faded, Brian asked if someone would lead us in prayer. A man stepped forward. We bowed our heads as he prayed—for protection on the road ahead, for wisdom and strength, and for unity across America.

Then came the drivers' meeting—routes, rest stops, safety reminders. A fuel company had donated five thousand gallons of diesel and gas, so our first destination would be a nearby station off I-40. Afterward we'd push east toward Kingman, Flagstaff, and the New Mexico line.

When the briefing ended, a few people led us in *God Bless America* and *Amazing Grace*. Engines idled low beneath the singing, harmonizing like a heartbeat.

I'd already mounted three flags on the back of my truck—Old Glory in the center, the *Don't Tread on Me* flag on one side, and a POW/MIA flag on the other. The morning wind caught them, snapping sharp against the blue Arizona sky. I took one last walk around my truck, checked my tires and lights, and climbed into the cab.

The CB crackled to life. "Convoy, get ready to roll."

We pulled out in formation, slow and steady, a line of chrome and steel stretching as far as I could see. Local deputies blocked intersections as we merged onto the highway. Families lined the frontage roads waving flags and homemade signs. Kids on their parents' shoulders pumped their fists in the air, motioning for us to blow our horns.

I laid on the air horn—and the others followed suit. The sound was thunder rolling across the desert.

Bridge after bridge was filled with patriots waving flags, holding signs, clapping as we passed. Fire departments parked their engines with ladders raised high. Ambulances and tow trucks flashed their lights in salute. It wasn't anger we saw on those faces—it was pride, and maybe a little relief that someone, finally, was standing up.

We slowed through Kingman, waving and honking to people who'd come out with banners that read *We Stand for Freedom*, *Stop the Steal*, and others. Then came Flagstaff—snow still on the ground, people bundled up and cheering from the bridges. In Winslow, an old man in a cowboy hat stood alone by the roadside, holding a flag as big as he was. I honked, and he raised it high, saluting as we passed.

Our speed rarely topped forty-five, but none of us cared. This wasn't about getting somewhere fast—it was about showing the world that the American spirit still had wheels under it.

As the sun began to set behind us, the desert sky turned to fire—orange fading to violet, the convoy's headlights stretching for miles. I remember looking in the mirror and seeing hundreds of rigs glowing in the twilight, rolling together like one heartbeat across the highway.

By the time darkness fell, the chatter on the CB had quieted to a hum of check-ins and directions. We were tired but wired—fueled by purpose.

We finally pulled off near the Arizona–New Mexico line, deep in **Navajo Nation.** The temperature had dropped to single digits, the air sharp and dry. We parked on an old frontage road beside a long-abandoned gas station—just cracked pavement and broken signs, the kind of place you'd miss if not for the line of headlights stretching into the distance.

But that night, it came to life.

Bonfires burned in metal barrels and pits around the old station lot. Locals from the nearby Navajo communities had come down to meet us. They'd set up tables with fry bread, Indian tacos, beans, and pork. The smell of food cut through the cold like a promise.

I'll never forget one elderly Navajo woman—small, silver-haired, probably in her eighties—standing in the bitter cold behind a large pot of beans. She wore what looked like handmade gloves with the fingertips cut off. I handed her my plate, and she looked up with a warm smile.

"You're doing a good thing," she said softly, ladling a generous scoop onto my plate. Her voice carried the calm strength of someone who'd lived through hard times and learned to meet them with grace.

I thanked her and sat by one of the fires with a few other drivers. We ate and talked with the Navajo families who had come out to welcome us. One man told us about his grandfather, who had driven trucks during the war, hauling supplies for the military. "He'd be proud of this," he said.

The cold was bitter—only nine degrees—but the fires and conversation kept us warm. Some drivers gave kids small flag stickers, others let them sit in the cabs to blow the horns. There was laughter, storytelling, even a few songs sung quietly under the stars.

I looked around and saw people from every walk of life—truckers, farmers, veterans, and Native American families—all gathered together, not divided by politics or background, but united by something simple and sacred: the belief that freedom was still worth fighting for.

Later that night, I stepped away from the fires and looked out across the lot. The trucks stretched out in both directions, red taillights and amber clearance lights glowing through the cold air, engines idling softly. The American flags we'd raised earlier now fluttered in the moonlight, shadows dancing on the pavement.

The wind carried faint laughter from the fires, the crackle of flames, the low growl of diesel engines that never fully rest.

I realized then that what we were building wasn't just a protest—it was a movement of hearts.

Under that wide desert sky, surrounded by strangers who already felt like family, I understood what freedom really sounded like. It wasn't noise or rebellion. It was the steady hum of conviction—the quiet unity of people who refused to quit.

That night, I climbed into my sleeper, the sound of the wind against the cab like a lullaby. The cold crept in around the edges, but I didn't care. I felt something I hadn't felt in years—**hope.**

This convoy had started as a drive for freedom. But now, it was becoming something greater—proof that the American spirit still burned bright, even in the darkest night.

Chapter 8 – Waking the Nation

The third morning of the convoy began with a cold wind cutting across the Navajo plains. I woke in my sleeper to the quiet hum of idling engines and the faint smell of campfire drifting through the cracked window. The sun hadn't fully risen yet, but the horizon was already glowing pink over the mesas. It was one of those mornings that reminded you why truckers fall in love with the open road—harsh, raw, and beautiful.

I climbed down from my sleeper and crossed the frontage road toward the old gas station where the Navajo families had gathered the night before. The lead truck sat nearby, its flatbed trailer once again doubling as a stage. Drivers were gathering around, bundled in jackets and hats, breath steaming in the cold.

Brian Brase's voice rang out across the lot, calling everyone together. What had started as a spontaneous morning tradition was becoming something sacred—an opening ceremony to each new day.

Several of the Navajo families had returned that morning, bringing with them trays of food: breakfast burritos, coffee, and fry bread still warm from the fire. Among them was a small group of elders, quiet and dignified, standing beside the flatbed as Brian led the Pledge of Allegiance. A hundred hands went to a hundred hearts. The sound of our voices echoing against the desert hills was haunting and powerful.

After the pledge, one of the elders offered a prayer in both English and Navajo—a beautiful blend of reverence and resilience. Then the Vice President of the Navajo Nation stepped forward. He was a tall man with a calm, steady voice, and when he spoke, the crowd fell silent.

He talked about the Navajo love for this country—the land, the freedom, the responsibility that comes with both. He spoke of the Code Talkers of World War II, how their language had helped win battles in the Pacific, and how the Navajo people had always stood shoulder to shoulder with America in times of trial.

"What you are doing," he said, gesturing to the convoy around us, "is needed. You remind the people that freedom requires courage. And courage begins with truth."

His words hit me hard. There was no politics in his tone—just conviction, the kind that can only come from experience and loss. When he stepped down, the crowd broke into applause, some wiping tears from their faces.

As the drivers began returning to their rigs, I crossed the highway to a small truck stop run by the tribe—a place called Speedy's. I grabbed a cup of coffee and was about to walk back when I noticed a man standing in front of my truck, just staring at it.

He looked to be in his forties, maybe older, wearing a ball cap pulled low. When he saw me, he froze, and then his eyes filled with tears.

"You're Grey Wolf, I found you," he said, voice shaking.

For a moment I wasn't sure how to respond. Grey Wolf was the handle I'd used on the CB for decades, a name that had become second nature. I nodded slowly. "Yeah, that's me."

He stepped closer, emotion spilling out as he spoke. "I was watching YouTube from my home near Sacramento. I saw one of your interviews, and something you said—it hit me. I told my wife, 'That man's right. That's a real man.' And though I was not planning on joining the convoy, I packed up my car and drove straight through to find, meet you, and shake your hand."

I didn't know what to say. The man was crying openly now, talking about how he'd lost faith in what America had become but seeing the convoy gave him hope again. I put a hand on his shoulder and told him I'd carry his message with me all the way to Washington. He gripped my hand and said, "Don't let them forget us."

We hugged before parting ways. As I crossed back over the highway, I thought about how one conversation, one spark, can ripple farther than we ever realize.

Soon after, it was time to roll out. Engines rumbled to life across the lot, drivers checking tires and lights. The morning air filled with the sound of air brakes and diesel chatter. We were lining up for Day Three, the convoy stretching nearly a mile down the road.

We hit the interstate again—forty, maybe forty-five miles an hour, same as the days before. The road ahead shimmered in the cold desert light. Every bridge we passed was packed with people waving flags and cheering. Some held signs that read We Stand With You or Freedom Isn't Free, and "We Love Truckers".

In every town we passed, it felt like more Americans were waking up.

Truckers not part of the convoy found our CB channel and asked to join. "You got room for one more?" they'd say. The answer was always the same: "Absolutely." Those who couldn't join stayed in the fast lane, honking and waving as they passed.

By the time we reached Albuquerque, the show of support was overwhelming. Every single bridge had people—hundreds of them—flags snapping in the wind. Fire trucks and ambulances parked on overpasses, lights flashing, horns sounding in salute. For miles, it felt like driving through a living river of red, white, and blue.

When we were about thirty minutes west of Tucumcari, a message came over the radio. The mayor herself—Ruth Litchfield—had invited the convoy to detour through town. We slowed, exited the interstate, and followed the old Route 66 toward the city center.

Downtown Tucumcari looked like a scene from another time—retro neon signs, murals of cowboys and desert sunsets, and locals lining the sidewalks waving flags. We spread two wide down the middle of the main road so regular traffic could still move, but everywhere we looked, people were cheering, crying, clapping.

The lead truck pulled into a vacant lot downtown where the mayor and several officers were waiting. She stood on the flatbed, smiling through tears as she spoke. "Our town's been quiet for years," she said. "But today—today you brought Tucumcari back to life."

Not everyone shared her enthusiasm. One man nearby began shouting angrily, waving his arms and demanding that we leave. But no one engaged. He marched up to a police cruiser, yelling at the officer inside to make us go. The officer stayed seated, calm and unmoved, and replied through the open window, "The mayor invited them. They're staying.

We spent about an hour there before Brian gave the signal to roll out again. The horns blasted in unison—a chorus of diesel thunder—and we made our way back to I-40 eastbound, bound for our next stop: Russell's Truck and Travel Center, near the Texas border.

The sun was sinking low as we drove, the desert sky fading from orange to violet while the convoy's headlights stretched into infinity. After a long, steady push, we finally rolled into Russell's just as the last glimmers of sunlight danced across the horizon—one final shimmer before the day gave way to night.

The parking lot filled quickly, a line of chrome and steel glinting under the floodlights. Inside, the smell of food and coffee hit like comfort. The staff at Russell's had been expecting us—the restaurant was fully staffed, showers were stocked and clean, and they even offered discounted fuel for convoy members.

I grabbed a seat at the counter inside and ordered dinner with a few other drivers. The place was packed wall to wall, voices buzzing with stories from the road. Halfway through the meal, a couple walked in—a man and his wife from Denver. They stood near the counter and raised their hands for attention.

"We just wanted to say thank you," the man said, his voice loud enough to cut through the chatter. "You're standing up for all of us. Dinner's on us tonight."

The room erupted in applause. Some people cheered, others wiped away tears.

A few minutes later, I spotted another familiar face—Duane Olinger from Mystery at Blind Frog Ranch. He'd driven over from his home near Amarillo to meet the convoy and was chatting with several people about how even border patrol agents he'd spoken with supported what we were doing. Duane mentioned that he and his wife had brought a batch of homemade breakfast burritos for the convoy. I introduced him to Brian, who was sitting nearby, and after a quick conversation between them, Duane and his wife began handing out burritos to anyone who wanted one—warm food and kind smiles passing through the crowd like sunlight breaking the chill.

It was one of those moments that made you realize this movement wasn't just about truckers anymore—it was about everyone.

Later that night, after I'd eaten and taken a long, hot shower, I stepped outside. The air was cold and there was a bit of frozen drizzle on my truck windows. A few drivers stood around their rigs talking quietly. From where I stood, I could see the faint glow of Texas lights on the horizon.

I leaned against my truck and looked up at the stars. It had been a long, emotional day—filled with pride, gratitude, and a sense that something much bigger than us was in motion.

I wondered what the next day would bring. Would our numbers grow? Would more towns come out to meet us?

The questions hung in the air as I climbed back into my sleeper, the soft ticking of the cooling engine echoing in the quiet night.

As I closed my eyes, one thought stayed with me: America was waking up.

And we were leading the way.

Chapter 9 – Oklahoma Rising (The Road to Elk City)

The morning at Russell's Truck and Travel Center began before dawn. I woke to the sound of air brakes hissing and the low hum of idling engines outside. Inside the cab, the cold crept in through the seams, nudging me awake. I slid on my boots, grabbed my hat, and stepped down onto the dirt lot. The air was crisp and still, tinted pink by the first light over the Texas line.

A handful of drivers were already up, stretching, rubbing the sleep from their eyes. Most of us drifted toward the truck-stop diner. The smell of fresh coffee hit before the door even closed behind me. Inside, the chatter was easy—talk of weather, the road ahead, and the long haul we had waiting for us. A few of us grabbed sandwiches, bottled water, and extra supplies for the miles to come. It felt like the quiet before the next push east.

When everyone had gathered outside again, Brian Brase called us over to the flatbed trailer that served as our makeshift stage. He thanked Russell's for hosting us and reminded everyone that safety came first, then nodded for us to begin the day the way we always did—with the Pledge of Allegiance and a prayer. Dozens of hands went to hearts, voices carrying across the lot as the sun crept higher above the horizon.

After the prayer, the drivers' meeting began: route details, rest stops, and reminders about spacing and speed. When it wrapped up, the engines rumbled back to life, one after another, and we rolled to the pumps. Russell's had opened every lane and was offering discounted fuel for the convoy. The smell of diesel filled the cool morning air as we topped off our tanks and checked lights and tires one last time.

Only then did the CB crackle to life: "Convoy, get ready to roll east."

We eased back onto Interstate 40, heading toward Texas, the line stretching behind us farther than the eye could see. It was the fourth day of the People's Convoy, and the energy was stronger than ever.

Within minutes of crossing into Texas, the support began again— bridge after bridge filled with patriots waving flags, families cheering, veterans saluting. Fire departments parked their trucks across overpasses, banners hanging high. Tow trucks lined the shoulders, lights flashing in red, white, and blue. You couldn't drive a mile without seeing a flag, a smile, or a salute.

Before Amarillo, something extraordinary happened. The land flattened out into that endless Texas plain, and for nearly ten miles straight, both sides of the highway were lined with people. Ten solid miles of patriots—standing in fields, on fences, on rooftops, waving flags and homemade signs. Some ran from their houses as we approached, flags in hand, desperate not to miss us. The sight of it hit me in the chest like a wave.

This wasn't about anger anymore. It wasn't about mandates or politics. It was about America remembering itself.

The radio crackled with chatter from excited drivers and local law enforcement. We were told that officials in Amarillo had set up a large area north of the interstate where we could stop for a short rally. We exited the freeway and wound our way into a wide dirt lot surrounded by cheering crowds.

The engines idled as people gathered around. The flatbed stage was already set, flags whipping in the wind. Brian Brase climbed up first, greeted by a roar of cheers. He spoke briefly, thanking the people of Amarillo for their spirit and for feeding the convoy along the way.

Next up was Leigh Dundas, a civil-rights attorney from Southern California who had been with us since day one and had become one of the convoy's strongest voices. She was fiery, sharp, and fearless—a woman who'd spent years fighting for medical freedom and personal rights, and who never hesitated to speak truth to power. Her voice cut through the wind like a blade. "Freedom isn't something the government gives you," she said. "It's something you were born with. And if we don't stand now, we risk losing it forever."

The crowd erupted in applause. You could feel the conviction in her words—the kind that burns long after the sound fades. I heard people saying, "She should run for President."

Then Dr. Paul Alexander took the mic. His tone was calm and deliberate, the voice of reason in a storm. He spoke about truth, science, and integrity, reminding everyone why this convoy mattered.

"This is not about politics," he said. "This is about restoring the voice of the people."

Local officials spoke next, thanking us for reminding their communities what unity looked like. People hugged, cried, and shook hands. It was hope made visible.

As Brian closed the rally, he raised his voice above the wind. "We need to remind them—" he shouted. The crowd thundered back as one: "YOU WORK FOR US!"

Just before we rolled out, a constable from the next county arrived in his marked SUV. After a short conversation with the organizers, he took position at the front of the convoy, lights flashing. For the next fifty miles, he led us east at a steady forty-five miles per hour. The sight of that lawman guiding a convoy of patriots through the plains—it was pure Americana.

When we reached the county line, he accelerated ahead, pulled onto the shoulder, and stopped. As we passed, he got out of his vehicle, removed his hat, and snapped to a full military salute.

The CB went silent. For a moment, no one spoke. The only sound was the deep hum of hundreds of diesel engines rolling past and the steady flap of flags in the wind. It was one of those moments that transcend words—where everyone feels the same thing without having to say it.

Crossing into Oklahoma, it felt like the convoy had taken on a life of its own. What started as a handful of trucks from California was now a river of Americans rolling east. The show of support didn't slow—it grew stronger. Oklahoma State Troopers were waiting at the border, lights flashing, and they waved us through in formation. At the first weigh station, troopers stood shoulder to shoulder outside their cruisers, giving thumbs-up and salutes. They'd even shut down the scale house so the convoy could roll through unimpeded.

Every bridge was filled with supporters—families, farmers, veterans, young and old alike. You could tell by their faces that this wasn't a protest to them; it was a promise. A reminder that Americans hadn't forgotten each other.

As the day wore on, the CB filled with chatter from volunteers helping manage spacing and from truckers joining in along the way. The sun arced high and then began to sink westward again, casting long shadows over the highway.

When we reached Exit 40 in Elk City, the line slowed. Up ahead, the road was lined with people—hundreds of them—standing shoulder to shoulder, waving flags and cheering as the convoy approached. The closer we got, the more it looked like the whole town had turned out.

We turned off the frontage road and made a sharp right into the SFI yard, an old trucking lot that had been opened for us. The lot was packed with volunteers, food tables, and even a few food trucks. Those hauling trailers pulled to the back while bobtail trucks like mine parked near the front. The sound of air brakes, laughter, and country music filled the air.

The people of Oklahoma had brought it.

Homemade meals lined the tables—casseroles, barbecue, chili, and cornbread. There were pies, cookies, and hot coffee by the gallon. Local families stood behind the tables, serving food with smiles and handshakes. "Thank you for standing up," one woman told me, ladling stew into a bowl. "We've needed this for a long time."

Kids ran between the trucks waving little flags. A church group handed out bottled water and blankets. Someone had even brought a portable speaker and was playing "God Bless the USA."

It wasn't just a stop—it was a celebration.

As the sun dropped below the horizon, the glow of headlights and floodlights lit the yard. Brian Brase climbed back up onto the flatbed to thank the community. A local pastor led a prayer, his voice steady and strong over the hum of idling engines. People bowed their heads, hats pressed to chests, the wind carrying his words into the night.

When the prayer ended, someone began to sing "Amazing Grace." One voice at first, then a dozen, then hundreds. It rolled through the yard like a wave—deep, resonant, and pure. Drivers, volunteers, and townspeople all joined in. For a few moments, time stood still.

Afterward, I walked along the line of trucks, talking with other drivers. Some were eating, some were fixing gear, some were just staring off at the horizon, quiet and reflective. Every one of us knew we were part of something bigger than ourselves.

Later that night, as I settled into my sleeper, I could still hear laughter outside, the murmur of voices, and the occasional honk of a truck horn. The Oklahoma wind rocked the cab gently, carrying the faint scent of smoke and barbecue.

Lying there, I thought about everything we'd seen that day—the flags, the people, the constable's salute, the food, the song. It was America in its purest form: ordinary people standing together for something extraordinary.

As my eyes grew heavy, one thought stayed with me.

If this was day four, I couldn't help wondering what the next sunrise would bring—what new miles, new faces, and new faith in America might rise with it.

Chapter 10 – The Eagle Over Big Cabin

Dawn came early in Elk City, a dull gray blanket stretching over the SFI yard.

A chill wind swept across the open lot, stirring the flags still mounted on the trucks from the night before. I climbed down from my sleeper and looked around—steam rising from idling stacks, volunteers moving between tables, the smell of coffee and sausage already in the air.

The people of Oklahoma had shown up again. Local families brought hot breakfast—biscuits, eggs, bacon, and more coffee than we could drink. They'd come to see us off, just like they had come to see us arrive the night before, with that same warm hospitality that never asked for anything in return.

As the sun began to climb, Brian Brase called everyone over to the flatbed stage. The crowd gathered close, hands in pockets, hats pulled low against the wind. We started the morning as we always did—with the Pledge of Allegiance, hundreds of voices rising together against the open sky. Then came a prayer, simple and heartfelt, asking for safety, strength, and wisdom as we rolled east.

The morning felt different, though—charged somehow. There was a deeper unity settling in, a sense that what had started as a spark was becoming a flame.

When Brian finished, Leigh Dundas stepped forward. She was a civil-rights attorney from Southern California, small in stature but powerful behind a microphone. Her voice carried like a battle cry, fierce and unwavering.

"History will remember who stood up," she said, her voice echoing across the lot. "And it will remember who stayed silent." She spoke about truth and accountability; about the courage it takes to stand when others bow. She wasn't just speaking to us—she was speaking for us. For every person who'd ever been told to sit down and stay quiet.

Her words drew cheers and a few tears. You could see people straightening their shoulders as she spoke, reminded of why they were there.

Next, Dr. Paul Alexander stepped up. His delivery was calm but commanding, the voice of a man grounded in conviction. He thanked the volunteers who'd been feeding and supporting the convoy, then spoke about freedom—not as a slogan, but as a moral obligation.

"The truth is not partisan," he said. "It belongs to the people. And the people must protect it."

Then came Josh Yoder of Freedom Flyers, a pilot representing others across the country who'd lost their jobs for refusing the mandates. His presence brought a wave of emotion through the crowd. He spoke not only for pilots, but for doctors, nurses, teachers—people forced to choose between their livelihood and their conscience. Some who complied, he said, suffered serious medical complications after. Fear had replaced freedom.

The lot went silent except for the steady hum of idling engines. When Josh finished, the applause was long and heartfelt. It wasn't about politics anymore; it was about humanity.

Afterward, the volunteers who'd been serving breakfast came forward with trays for the drivers who hadn't eaten yet. Someone began to sing *Amazing Grace* again, and others joined in, voices blending with the wind. The sound rolled across the lot like a benediction.

When the last note faded, Brian gave the signal to roll. Engines came alive one by one, air brakes hissing as the line formed. The convoy eased out of the SFI yard and back onto the frontage road, heading east toward Oklahoma City.

The day stretched long and steady. Each mile carried the same rhythm—the hum of engines, the chatter of CB radios, the steady pulse of purpose. As we rolled through the heart of Oklahoma, every overpass seemed alive with flags and people. Families waved, veterans saluted, and kids held homemade signs. Even a single person standing alone with a flag meant something—it said, *We see you. We're with you.*

As we approached Oklahoma City, coordination got tricky. Not every vehicle had a CB radio, and messages had to be relayed through hand signals, phone calls, or word of mouth. Some drivers missed exits, others fell back, but the Oklahoma State Troopers were there every step of the way. They helped regroup the stragglers, guiding them back into formation.

Their support was something to see—patrol cars lined up at interchanges, lights flashing, troopers waving as we passed. They weren't just managing traffic—they were showing solidarity.

We bypassed the main stretch of the city and caught Interstate 44 northeast toward Joplin, Missouri. Word came over the CB that we'd be stopping for the night at a place called Big Cabin, near the intersection of I-44 and the Will Rogers Turnpike. The name felt fitting—Big Cabin, the heart of Oklahoma.

The afternoon sun dipped low behind us, turning the sky gold and red. The convoy moved as one long, unbroken line of chrome and color, each rig bearing its own banners and flags. We'd been rolling for hours, the kind of miles that wear on both man and machine. But as the sun fell low, every ache vanished at what we saw ahead.

When we exited the interstate, the sight waiting ahead took my breath away.

Thousands of people had gathered in Big Cabin. They lined the roads, the overpasses, the parking lots. Flags waved from pickups, tractors, even horseback riders. Volunteers had set up food tents and tables. It felt like the whole state had come out to welcome us.

We pulled into a large empty dirt lot next to a travel-center, where organizers and local volunteers had arranged space for the trucks. I parked near a towering statue of a Native warrior that watched over the grounds. As I climbed out, I was hit by a wave of noise—cheers, laughter, the sound of live country music from a flatbed stage nearby.

The smell of grilled beef and onions filled the air. Volunteers were flipping burgers, stirring chili, and serving plates piled high with local ranch beef. "All donated," one woman said proudly as she handed me a burger. "Oklahoma's feeding you tonight."

I stood there for a moment, taking it in—the sound, the smell, the sheer energy of it all. Then something strange caught my ear—a sharp cry, almost like a whistle. I looked up into the orange sky, squinting against the light.

And there it was—a bald eagle, circling low above me.

Its wings caught the last glow of the sunset, turning in slow, deliberate arcs above the flags and trucks—as if keeping watch. The air seemed to still around it. Every few seconds, the bird would bank, the sun lighting its feathers like burnished gold.

I stared, unable to look away. The woman behind the grill noticed me watching and laughed. "You even have an eagle with you tonight?" she asked.

I smiled and said, "Is he here often?"

She shook her head slowly, her voice soft but certain. "No, sir. He flew in with you."

I stood there, eyes still on the sky, knowing I'd just seen something that words couldn't quite explain.

Chapter 11 – The Road to Cuba (Day Seven)

Morning came quietly in Big Cabin, the sky pale and washed with silver light. The air was cool—the kind that wakes you before you're ready. Engines idled low across the travel center lot, a steady hum beneath the sound of distant voices and clattering coffee cups. It was our seventh day on the road, and even though the miles were starting to wear on us, the spirit of the convoy was still strong.

I walked into the Big Cabin Travel Center, grabbed a hot coffee and a couple of bottles of soda for the day ahead, and spent a few minutes talking with other drivers doing the same. New faces had started showing up each morning—people who'd driven from nearby towns just to see us off or join in for a few miles. Every day brought more of them. And every morning, I caught myself wondering, *What will this day bring?*

Our destination that day was Cuba, Missouri—an old truck stop off Interstate 44 called Dottie's. Today, it's a Travel Centers of America (TA), but back in February 2022, it was still Dottie's. We'd been told it was a big stop with plenty of space for the growing convoy, which was good—because we were going to need it.

By sunrise, Brian Brase and the co-organizers were already setting up on the stage. Beside him stood Marcus Sommers, another key voice helping manage logistics and communication between the rigs and support vehicles. Together, they'd become the backbone of the movement—different personalities, same mission.

We started the morning, as always, with the Pledge of Allegiance. Hundreds of hands went to hearts, voices rising into the Oklahoma air. It had become more than a ritual; it was our compass. Afterward, a volunteer led us in prayer—simple words asking for safe travels, good judgment, and humble hearts on the road ahead.

Then came something new. A man stepped up onto the stage—a poet, though I can't recall his name—and began to read. His poem wasn't loud or dramatic; it was steady and thoughtful, like the land itself. He spoke about freedom, sacrifice, and the road as a symbol of endurance. When he finished, the crowd stood in silence for a moment before breaking into applause.

Then Brian took the mic. He thanked the poet, then looked out over the line of trucks ready to roll.

"We're more than drivers now," he said. "We're messengers. Every mile we roll, we're reminding America that the people still matter."

He paused, letting the words settle. Then, raising his voice again, he shouted, "Who do they work for?"

With a thunderous roar, the crowd answered in unison, "They work for us!"

The echo rolled across the lot like thunder, bouncing off the trucks and into the open sky. It wasn't just noise—it was conviction.

With that, Brian gave the signal. Engines roared to life, air brakes hissed, and we began to line up. The morning sun was just cresting over the trees as we pulled onto I-44 eastbound.

But something was off.

Where was Mike Landis—one of the lead organizers and the driver of the lead truck? I wondered as we rolled east. That question would be answered later.

Almost immediately, the horns started—a deep, rolling sound that could've shaken the heavens. Flags lined every overpass, just like the days before—but there were more now. So many more. American flags, state flags, even Canadian flags—some paired together, stitched side by side. I remember seeing one flag where the Maple Leaf and the Stars and Stripes waved as one, snapping in the wind.

It was like something biblical—the horns of Jericho echoing across the plains.

For a while, I rode in silence, just watching the people on the bridges —waving, saluting, holding signs that said things like *We Love Our Truckers* and *Freedom Is Essential*. Each honk, each wave, felt like fuel for the heart. Every person in that convoy was sacrificing something for this movement.

The day's drive was long and steady. Convoy cars and motorcycles had to stop more often for fuel, while the big rigs could roll for miles. We'd slow now and then to let them catch up, the line stretching out like a silver ribbon across the Oklahoma hills. Volunteers along the route radioed updates, letting us know which fuel stops were open for supporters and which were reserved for the main line.

When we crossed into Missouri, the landscape changed—rolling hills, wooded valleys, and the first signs of spring budding on the trees. The bridges were still packed. Families waved from porches and pastures. Flags hung from tractors, barns, and fences. You could see it in their faces—this wasn't about politics anymore. It was about connection. About being seen.

As we neared Cuba, traffic thickened. People had begun parking along the shoulders miles before the exit, waving flags and shouting encouragement. The smell of barbecue and wood smoke drifted through the air.

We exited the interstate and crossed the overpass toward the north side of I-44, where Dottie's Truck Stop sat gleaming in the setting sun. The lot was already packed. People were everywhere—lining the entry, the overpasses, the grass shoulders—waving and cheering as the convoy rolled in.

It took time to get everyone parked. The organizers' bus was always first in behind the lead truck, then the core convoy drivers. I pulled my bobtail into line near the front, just a few spots back, the familiar sound of air brakes and laughter filling the air.

A local politician—his name escapes me now—was waiting near the entrance, shaking hands and welcoming drivers. He spoke briefly during that evening's rally, thanking us for reminding people what civic courage looked like.

Every evening followed a familiar rhythm: a short rally, Q&A, route updates, prayer, and fellowship. Reporters moved through the crowd, interviewing drivers, volunteers, and families. Some of the stories they captured were emotional—testimonies of loss, resilience, and renewed hope.

That day's drive had been one of quiet reflection for me. Not less meaningful—just quieter. The sights were the same—the flags, the tears, the cheers—but inside, I felt calm. It was as if the movement had found its rhythm, and I was learning to listen to it.

The staff at Dottie's were incredible. They worked hard to keep up with the surge of people. Even with all the homemade food spread out across the lot—pies, casseroles, cakes, and crockpots filled with chili—I decided to eat inside the diner. I wanted a hot plated meal and a chance to sit with other drivers and volunteers.

The restaurant was packed, the hum of voices filling every corner. Locals came up to shake hands, take photos, or thank us for what we were doing. A few even asked for autographs—something that still caught me off guard. We weren't celebrities; we were citizens. But in that moment, it felt like America was remembering its everyday heroes again.

After dinner, I stepped outside. The night air was cool, and floodlights washed the trucks in soft white light. The smell of grilled food still lingered, and people milled around sharing stories and laughter.

Back at my truck, I decided to do a little organizing. I had hundreds of paper lunch bags that supporters had handed out along the way— filled with snacks, cards, and letters. Some had started to tumble down from the upper bunk. I'd finally picked up a couple of plastic bins to store them better.

As I sorted through them, I noticed something unexpected. Inside some of the bags, along with cookies and chips, were folded envelopes with small cash donations—fives, tens, twenties, and even a fifty or two. I hadn't realized people were quietly giving money along with their notes.

Some of the fruit had gone bad in a few of the older bags, so I tossed those, separating the rest into piles—snacks in one bin, letters and drawings in another, and cash donations into a large envelope.

It felt good to bring some order to the chaos—a kind of road-time spring cleaning. As I worked, I read a few of the notes. Some were written in careful cursive, others in crayon. One from a child said simply,

Thank you for driving for my dad. Another from an elderly couple read, *We pray for you every night. Keep going.*

By the time I finished, the lot had quieted. The hum of engines had softened, fading into the distance. I climbed into my sleeper and sat for a moment, looking through the window at the long line of trucks bathed in soft light.

It struck me then that this journey wasn't just about protest or politics—it was about faith. Not just faith in God, but faith in people, in each other, in the idea that unity could still exist.

I leaned back on my bunk and listened to the faint echoes of laughter outside. The night was calm and still. My hands smelled faintly of diesel and coffee, and I smiled, thinking about how far we'd come— from the dust of California to the heart of Missouri.

As I drifted toward sleep, I thought about the letters, the faces, the voices that shouted *God Bless America* from the bridges.

Each one was a reminder that the spirit of this country—tired or not —was still alive and moving.

Tomorrow, we'd roll again.

Chapter 12 – The Flag

Morning broke cool and quiet over Cuba, Missouri. The air had that early-spring bite to it—the kind that wakes you up before the coffee does. I climbed out of my sleeper, stretched, and looked across the lot at Dottie's Truck Stop. The familiar hum of idling engines filled the air, mingling with the smell of bacon, diesel, and wood smoke.

It felt good to have an organized truck again. The night before, I'd finally gone through the mountain of brown paper bags and notes supporters had handed me since California—cleaned up the fruit, sorted the snacks, and tucked the letters and cash donations neatly away. There was something peaceful about waking up to order after so many days of motion and noise.

Inside Dottie's, the diner was already busy. Drivers sat shoulder to shoulder at the counter, sipping coffee and trading stories while the morning news flickered on the television overhead. Most of the coverage was about the war in Ukraine. I remember staring at the screen, thinking how quickly the world had shifted—from the optimism of President Trump's first term to the uncertainty and division that now filled the headlines.

As I watched, I thought about all the people I'd met since leaving California—the ones on the bridges waving flags, the families lining the roads, the veterans saluting as we passed. I wondered what went through their minds when they saw us roll by. Maybe they were thinking the same thing I was: that this country needed to find its way back to what made it great in the first place.

I finished my coffee, nodded to the waitress, and stepped outside. The lot was alive with movement—drivers stretching, volunteers serving breakfast, supporters stopping by to shake hands or snap a quick photo. The morning drivers' meeting was about to start.

That's when I noticed it.

Sometime during the night, a new rig had appeared in the center of the lot—the lead truck, Mike Landis's flatbed, parked proudly with something massive mounted to its bed. A tall steel flagpole rose from the trailer, secured with chains and binders, and from it hung a great cotton flag—the old 48-star American flag, faded but beautiful, rippling gently in the breeze.

It wasn't there when I'd gone to bed.

I made my way closer just as Brian Brase called everyone together. The crowd gathered in front of the stage, hats off, hands to hearts. The Pledge of Allegiance rang out first, hundreds of voices rising in unison toward that flag fluttering above us. Then came the morning prayer—simple words of thanks and strength for the miles ahead.

When it ended, Brian turned the mic over to Mike Landis. He adjusted his hat, looked out across the crowd, and said, "Some of you might've noticed I wasn't with you yesterday."

A murmur rippled through the crowd.

"I got a call," he continued, his voice steady but low. "It was from the daughter of a World War II veteran who gave his life in battle. She told me she still had his casket flag—a 48-star flag—and she wanted it to fly with the convoy all the way to Washington, D.C." She said her father would want that, and would be with us if alive today.

He paused, letting that sink in. "She said, 'Just get it back to me when it's over—no matter what shape it's in. Tattered or not.'"

The crowd fell silent. You could hear the wind against the trucks, the faint hum of idling engines, the shuffling of boots on the pavement.

Mike went on to explain that after receiving the flag, he'd driven to Four States Trucks and Chrome Shop in Joplin, Missouri. The employees there had volunteered their time and materials to build the massive flagpole we were now looking at. They'd spent hours fabricating a base and mount that would hold the flag high above his flatbed—without ever letting it touch the trailer.

As he spoke, the morning light caught the fabric, the cotton threads glinting faintly gold. It wasn't just a flag—it was a symbol.

Mike finished quietly, his voice tight with emotion. "That flag flew before most of us were even born," he said. "But it still stands for everything we're fighting for."

You could've heard a pin drop. The crowd stood still, some with tears in their eyes, as the flag waved gently above us—a reminder of sacrifice, duty, and the weight of what freedom costs.

Then Brian stepped forward again and raised his voice. "Let's give that hero—and that family—the convoy he deserves."

Engines roared to life, air brakes hissed, and one by one, we lined up to roll east. The Missouri State Troopers had blocked the exits temporarily while they set up patrol cars farther down the interstate to secure our entry. When they waved us forward, the sound of a hundred diesel engines came together like thunder.

Just before pulling out, they paused. I set my brakes and stepped down for one last stretch. Across the grass near the truck stop exit, stood a young couple with two small children. The woman caught my eye, and I smiled, thinking they wanted a photo. But as she approached, tears began streaming down her face.

"Are you one of the drivers?" she asked.

"Yes, ma'am," I said softly.

She reached out with trembling hands, and before I knew it, she was hugging me, sobbing into my shoulder. Her husband came forward too, his eyes red. I wrapped an arm around both of them as they cried, the weight of their emotion pressing against me like a wave.

They told me they were scared—scared for their children, for the country, for the future. "We need this," the woman said through her tears. "We need to know America still has people like you."

As I held them, I looked over their shoulders at the children watching, frozen, unsure of what to do. I realized this would be a moment they'd never forget—the sight of their parents crying, hugging a total stranger, not out of fear, but out of hope.

When they finally pulled away, I promised them I'd carry their message all the way to Washington, D.C. "Consider me your Pony Express," I said with a small smile. "I'll make sure your voices get there."

It felt fitting, standing there in Missouri—the home of the Pony Express.

Moments later, the troopers waved us forward. I climbed back into my truck, set my coffee in the holder, and eased out onto the ramp. Behind me, the convoy stretched like a living river of chrome and color. The troopers had shut down the slow lane for several miles, giving us a clear path to merge.

As we gathered speed, the horns began—a deep, rolling chorus that seemed to shake the sky.

The further east we went, the stronger the support grew. Every bridge, every overpass was alive with people waving flags, holding signs, and saluting as we passed. It was hard to put into words what that kind of unity felt like—you could only feel it in your chest.

By the time we hit Illinois, word had already spread. Early in the convoy, we'd been told that Illinois authorities didn't want us traveling through on Interstate 70, that we should find another route. But patriots from across the state had gone straight to their governor's office, demanding the convoy be allowed to pass.

Eventually, they relented—but with a warning. We were told that any infraction, even the smallest one, would bring citations and delays. So we kept it tight, kept it respectful.

What happened next was something none of us expected.

As we crossed the state line, it was as if the entire state had turned out to welcome us. Bridge after bridge, ramp after ramp—people everywhere. Flags waving, horns blaring, the air alive with sound and color.

And then came the skies.

A crop duster appeared first, flying low along the highway, dipping its wings back and forth in salute. Then, in the distance, a white Huey helicopter came into view. Beneath it, suspended from its skids, was a massive American flag. The chopper swung out ahead of the convoy, then looped back over us, circling so that everyone could see.

The sight of it against the blue sky made my throat tighten. It was like something out of a movie—one of those moments that etch themselves into your soul.

As the Huey banked and circled, the CB chatter lit up. Drivers calling out, cheering, some choking up as they tried to talk. It was pride, pure and unfiltered, soaring above us in red, white, and blue.

By the time we neared Indiana, the sun was setting low, casting long shadows across the highway. My mirrors were filled with light—the golden glow of hundreds of headlights, a moving line of hope stretching clear to the horizon.

Illinois had made its stand that day.

Patriots—one.

Politicians—zero.

Chapter 13 – The Layover in Monrovia

Crossing into Indiana that evening, the road began to smooth out beneath our tires, and the horizon glowed faintly gold as the sun fell behind us. The air was cooler, gentler—almost like a reward for the miles behind us. We would be staying at the Ted Everett Farm Equipment location in Monrovia, Indiana. None of us knew much about the place, but we'd heard it was ready for us—food, parking, and space enough for every truck, car, RV, and motorcycle in the convoy.

By the time we exited the interstate, the signs were there—crowds gathered on the overpasses, headlights flashing, flags waving against the afternoon sky. As we turned off the main road and rolled toward the farm property, the sight ahead took my breath away.

The Ted Everett grounds stretched wide in every direction, with the big arena lit up like a beacon. Vendors lined the entrance road—food trucks, barbecue pits, tents, T-shirt and flag vendors, and locals waving as we passed. You could smell diesel, and grilled meat in the air.

We rolled in slowly, led by the organizers' bus. The grounds crew guided us with flashlights, parking rigs in neat lines across the gravel lots. Cars and RVs filled the front, while semis faced one another in long rows in the back, forming a wide open courtyard in the middle. When I stepped out of my cab, the place buzzed with life—families talking, and a sound that felt like a hometown festival.

The locals brought everything—homemade casseroles, cake, pies, coffee, and plenty of gratitude. It felt like stepping back into the America we all remembered: neighborly, honest, proud.

***

The Night of the Flag

As darkness settled in, a pickup rolled into the courtyard. Word spread fast—someone from Utah had brought something special: a new gold-fringed American flag. It wasn't just big—it was massive, something around fifty by a hundred feet of fabric gleaming beneath the floodlights like liquid silk.

The volunteers spread the flag across the open courtyard, dozens of hands gripping the edges, not allowing it to touch the ground. The man who'd brought it raised a bullhorn.

"Tonight," he said, "we're going to walk beneath this flag. As you do, think of someone who is special to you, who gave their life for this country. Think of what this flag means—not just to you, but to every generation that came before us."

Silence fell. The engines idled softly, the flag rippling in front of us. Then, one by one, people began walking beneath it. Some carried flashlights; others lifted their phones high, the light glowing through the fabric like stained glass. Faces appeared in that glow—some smiling, others in tears, all united.

I switched on my headlights with the rest of the convoy, bathing the courtyard in white light. Watching that massive flag move in front of us, it felt like we'd built a cathedral out of color and memory.

I thought about the couple I'd met in Cuba—their children watching as their parents wept—and about the daughter who'd given Mike Landis her father's burial flag. Moments like those had been the heart of this journey—reminders of why we rolled. Everything about this moment felt like a prayer—spoken not in words, but in unity.

A drone buzzed quietly overhead, capturing the sight: rows of chrome, hundreds of hands holding that banner high, every horn sounding like a hymn. When the last person passed beneath it, the volunteers folded the flag with reverence, never letting it touch the ground. The crowd erupted in cheers; horns roared again, a sound of reverence and pride mingled in the cold Indiana night.

When the echoes faded, stillness returned. People lingered, reluctant to leave the space where the flag had flown. Then the rhythm of evening came back—soft music from a flatbed, laughter between drivers, the smell of barbecue and hot dogs still drifting through the air.

That night, we gathered in small circles, sipping coffee and sharing stories. The talk was quieter now—about families, faith, and the road ahead. We knew that tomorrow, for the first time in days, we wouldn't drive. We would rest.

***

The Day of Rest

Morning came calm and cool, sunlight spilling across the courtyard. The air smelled of bacon and coffee. For once, there was no rush—just a quiet peace. Drivers sat in lawn chairs or tinkered with their rigs. It felt good to breathe, to simply exist without the next mile calling our name.

Later in the morning, Brian set up a stage in the center of the courtyard—a flatbed with a bullhorn. He stood tall and smiled. "If you've got a story to tell," he said, "this is your stage. Today, we listen."

One by one, people stepped forward. Some spoke in short bursts; others broke down halfway through. A nurse from Texas told how she'd lost her job after refusing the mandated shot. A young father from Ohio described nearly losing his business to the lockdowns. A mother shared how she'd been barred from her son's hospital room before he passed.

Every story cut deep. Every voice added another heartbeat to what the convoy had become—not a protest, but a living expression of resilience and healing.

***

The Grandfather and the Pocket Constitutions

Sometime that afternoon, as I was speaking with a few drivers in the courtyard, a man approached with his two grandchildren—a boy and a girl, both in their early teens. He smiled politely and said, "Grey Wolf, I'd consider it an honor if you'd give my grandkids these."

He handed me two small pocket Constitutions.

I nodded, took the booklets, then stood before them and handed each their own.

"Let's open to the Declaration of Independence," I said. "There's a passage here that tells you everything you need to know about why we're doing what we're doing."

They opened their booklets as I reached into my pocket and pulled out my own well-worn copy. Together, we turned to the same page. I began to read aloud:

"We hold these truths to be self-evident, that all men are created equal, that they are endowed by their Creator with certain unalienable Rights, that among these are Life, Liberty, and the pursuit of Happiness. That to secure these rights, Governments are instituted among Men, deriving their just powers from the consent of the governed. That whenever any Form of Government becomes destructive of these ends, it is the Right—yes, even the duty—of the People to alter or to abolish it."

I looked up from the page. "That's what this convoy is," I told them. "A reminder. A living message to those in power—that they work for us."

The kids nodded solemnly, clutching their booklets. Their grandfather's eyes glistened as he stepped forward and shook my hand. "Thank you," he said softly.

It was a brief exchange, but it carried the weight of generations. I'll never forget it.

***

The Evening Rally

By late afternoon, we gathered once more—this time inside the big arena. The bleachers were packed—drivers, families, locals, all shoulder to shoulder. The echoes of voices and applause filled the space.

Leigh Dundas had already returned home by then, but the stage was still full. Josh Yoder spoke with quiet strength, telling of pilots who'd lost their careers for standing their ground. Dr. Paul Alexander followed, his words steady and clear—bridging science with conviction. Then came Attorney General ToddRokita, the chief legal officer of the State of Indiana, a former U.S. Representative and Secretary of State who has made defending constitutional liberties a hallmark of his office. Then came Tyler Lee, Republican nominee for Congress in North Carolina's 12th District, a real-estate entrepreneur who had leveraged his candidacy into a broader message of citizen voice and accountability. Mike Landis and Marcus Sommers stood together on the flatbed, thanking everyone there for holding the line and reminding us that our journey wasn't just physical—it was moral.

"We're not finished," Mike said. "This isn't the end—it's the foundation."

Applause shook the rafters. The energy in that room felt less like celebration and more like commitment—a shared vow to keep going, no matter what came next.

When the rally ended, the crowd spilled outside into the cool night air. The sun had set, leaving a soft orange glow on the horizon. Kids ran in the distance waving small American flags, dogs barked playfully, and someone near the food tents strummed the chords of "Simple Man."

I stood for a while, looking across the field. The great flag from the night before was gone—carefully folded away—but its presence still seemed to hang in the air like a memory that refused to fade.

We had driven thousands of miles. We had shared food, prayers, and tears. And now, for a single day in Monrovia, Indiana, we rested—not because we were done, but because the road ahead still waited.

Tomorrow, the engines would roar again. And the People's Convoy would roll east once more.

Chapter 14 – Just One Day Away

The morning broke cold and gray over Monrovia, Indiana. The sun had barely started to lift above the tree line, its light soft and pale against the mist that hung low across the Ted Everett Farm Equipment lot. A thin layer of frost coated the trucks, catching the faint glint of dawn. The air carried that quiet stillness you only get in the Midwest before sunrise—a kind of peace that makes the sound of every engine and every footstep seem sharper.

Volunteers from the local community had already arrived, setting out coffee and boxes of donuts on folding tables. The smell drifted through the yard, warm and comforting against the chill. I wrapped my hands around a cup and took a slow sip, the heat soaking into my fingers. Around me, drivers stirred in their cabs, stretching, climbing down, rubbing their arms against the cold. The day ahead was heavy with meaning—just one more day before the one long run to Hagerstown, Maryland, our staging point before D.C. One more night on the road, and we'd be there.

As the sun began to rise, the light poured over the arena bleachers where we gathered for the morning meeting. It had become our daily ritual: the Pledge of Allegiance, a prayer, and the route briefing. But this one felt different. You could see it in the faces of the drivers, the families, even the volunteers who had come to see us off. We weren't just rolling out of another stop—we were heading into the final stretch of something far larger than any of us had imagined when this convoy first left California.

Flags waved from pickups along the fence line. People stood bundled in coats and hats, holding signs that read *We Believe* and *Keep Rolling for Freedom*. As I looked around, I saw the same guitarist who had played at nearly every departure, strumming his guitar near the exit, his breath visible in the cold air. Every note seemed to blend with the low hum of idling diesel engines.

When the meeting ended, we returned to our rigs. Engines roared to life one by one, the sound swelling like an orchestra tuning up before a show. A volunteer in a reflective vest waved the lead trucks forward, and the line began to move. We wound slowly through the turns leading out of the farm lot, the convoy stretching back farther than the eye could see. As we merged onto the on-ramp for Interstate 70, the state troopers held back traffic, giving us room to form up.

The radio crackled to life with familiar voices: "Convoy's rolling east. Keep it steady at 45." Each driver responded in turn. It was methodical now, smooth—a rhythm born from days of practice. We knew our spacing, our signals, our pace. Cars, RVs, and motorcycles fell into line behind the big rigs, their flags fluttering wildly in the morning wind.

Once on the highway, the full scale of what we had become was breathtaking. For mile after mile, our convoy filled the number two lane, a ribbon of chrome and color stretching to the horizon. Overpasses were crowded again—families waving flags, firefighters and police officers standing in salute, farmers with tractors parked by the fences. Everywhere we went, America seemed to show up.

Passing through Dayton, then Columbus, the crowds only grew. Some stood on rooftops, others waved from overpasses wrapped in blankets. Kids waved hand-painted signs that said *Thank You, Truckers!* and *Freedom Rides With You!* The horns answered in return—long, echoing blasts that rolled like thunder across the plains. It was something primal, a shared heartbeat between the road and the people watching from above.

The day stayed cold, the wind biting through the seams of the cab. By late afternoon, as we neared Cambridge, Ohio, the temperature dropped even further. I remember feeling the sting on my ears when I stepped out of the truck at our final stop of the day.

The town of Cambridge greeted us in full force. At the bottom of the off-ramp stood a Speedway gas station, its lights glowing against the gray sky. Behind it was an open lot—once part of an old truck stop, now cleared and waiting for us. Volunteers had already set up grills and tables. The smell of hotdogs and burgers cut through the cold air as we pulled in, one truck at a time, following the volunteers' hand signals into neat rows.

Across the road, other trucks parked at the Go-Mart. Mike Landis, in the lead truck, parked his rig on a slight rise behind the Speedway, high enough that you could see it from almost anywhere in the lot. The big flag he carried from the World War II veteran's family waved in the wind, its stars glowing softly in the floodlights. It was a sight that stopped people in their tracks.

That evening, we gathered for another rally near the back of the lot. Brian Brase climbed up on the flatbed, microphone in hand. The crowd huddled close, breath misting in the cold. He gave updates, shared a few words of encouragement, and reminded us that tomorrow would be our last push before Hagerstown. His voice carried a mix of fatigue and pride. We'd come thousands of miles. We'd endured breakdowns, long days, and cold nights. Now, we were just one day away.

A few reports came in over the radio—minor fender-benders, nothing serious—but it was a reminder of the risks of moving something this large, this coordinated. Still, the mood stayed upbeat. Volunteers passed out food, locals thanked drivers for standing up, and for a moment, the world outside the convoy faded away. It felt like family.

Later, as the crowd thinned, I walked across the lot, coffee in hand. The air was freezing, sharp enough to make your breath catch. But I didn't mind. The sound of laughter and conversation filled the night, and the glow from the trucks washed everything in soft amber light. The wind tugged at the flags above the rigs—American, POW-MIA, Gadsden—all fluttering together like a single, living thing.

I found myself thinking about the road ahead. Tomorrow we'd reach Hagerstown, just outside of Washington, D.C. The question that had lingered since California was still unanswered—what would happen when we got there? Would we drive into D.C.? Would we stay outside and hold ground? No one knew for sure. But as I looked around at the people gathered there—tired, cold, but united—I realized that maybe it didn't matter. Whatever came next, we had already done something incredible. We had reminded a nation what solidarity looked like.

Before heading to bed, I stopped near the volunteers' tables. One of them handed me a bowl of chili and a small American flag on a stick. "Keep it," she said. "It's just a little thing, but it means a lot." I tucked it into my dashboard cup holder where it would stay for the rest of the trip.

When I finally climbed into my sleeper, the hum of idling engines lulled me into a kind of trance. Through the window, I could still see Mike's truck on the hill, its flag waving strong against the dark sky. The stars above it seemed brighter that night, the air clearer, as if the land itself was holding its breath.

I leaned back, pulled the blanket up to my shoulders, and let out a long sigh. Tomorrow would be the last leg—the final run to Hagerstown, the edge of the nation's capital. After days of motion, miles of reflection, and a thousand small acts of kindness, we were almost there.

Just one day away. Every mile east was proof that the spirit of the people still moved.

As the engines cooled and the night settled over Cambridge, I lay awake listening to the wind slide past the cab. We were only one day from Hagerstown, but it already felt like the edge of something greater. Every mile east was more than distance — it was proof that the spirit of the people still moved, even through the cold and the dark.

Chapter 15 – Just One More Push (The Road to Hagerstown)

Morning broke cold and still over Cambridge, Ohio. A sliver of sunlight slipped through the curtain of my sleeper and landed square across my face, pulling me from a light sleep. I blinked, rolled over, and stared at the thin glow on the wall. *This is it,* I thought. The last push.

I sat up, the familiar creak of the bunk beneath me sounding louder than usual. The air inside the cab was cool, my breath faintly visible. Outside, engines were beginning to rumble to life, and voices carried faintly through the morning air. It was time to get ready. I started stowing away the few loose items I hadn't tied down—coffee mugs, notepads, and my logbook—so nothing would rattle or crash on the road ahead. Old habits from years on the road die hard.

Then came the next thought: coffee.

It was a long walk from where I'd parked the night before down to the Speedway station. For the first time since the convoy began, no volunteers had brought coffee to the lot that morning. So, I zipped up my jacket and started the trek, boots crunching across the frost-coated gravel. The air was crisp, biting, but it felt good.

When I reached the Speedway, I wasn't alone. A line of drivers stretched out the door—every one of us chasing that first cup. Truckers and coffee—it's more than routine; it's ritual. The smell hit me as soon as I walked in, rich and warm, cutting through the chill. I poured a cup, grabbed a few pastries, and lingered near the door, talking with a few other drivers. Nobody said it out loud, but everyone knew what day it was. The day we'd been chasing for nearly two weeks—the final run to Hagerstown, Maryland.

By the time I made my way back toward the lot, people were gathering near the flatbed stage of Mike Landis's lead truck. I weaved through the crowd, coffee in hand, and found a spot close to the front as Brian Brase stepped up to the microphone.

We began, as always, with the Pledge of Allegiance, voices strong even in the cold. Then a local pastor offered a short prayer for protection and wisdom. The silence that followed was heavy—like the air itself knew this wasn't just another morning.

Brian looked out over the crowd, his face serious. "We're heading into the home stretch," he said, "but we need to be mindful. They know we're coming. The National Guard's been called up around D.C. They're nervous. They think we're coming to cause trouble."

A low murmur spread through the crowd. Brian raised his hand for silence.

"We're not here for that," he said firmly. "We're here to represent the people—peacefully, respectfully, and with conviction. What we do today and tomorrow will define how the world sees us."

He paused, his gaze sweeping over the crowd. Then, with a sudden burst of energy, he raised the mic and shouted, "Who do they work for?"

The answer came like thunder—thousands of voices roaring back in unison:

"THEY WORK FOR US!"

He was right. January 6, 2021, was still fresh in everyone's minds—fresh in mine, too. I knew how easily things could be twisted, how quickly intentions could be painted in the darkest colors. D.C. wasn't like the rest of America. It was its own world—one hundred square miles of government and media, with its own rules, its own fears. One wrong move, one bad headline, and the message could be lost.

As Brian spoke, my mind drifted. I thought about the promises I'd made along the way—the hugs, the letters, the prayers. I wasn't just a driver anymore. None of us were. We were representatives now—not elected, but chosen by the hearts of the people who'd handed us those flags and notes and asked us to carry their voices east. We were messengers. And in some strange way, I felt like we carried more moral weight than those inside the Capitol itself.

I thought about what I'd told the kids in Monrovia—that we were a constitutional republic, not a democracy. That our freedoms were not granted by government but protected from it. The words of the

Declaration of Independence still echoed in my head: *"Governments are instituted among men, deriving their just powers from the consent of the governed."*

That was what this was about—consent. Representation. Liberty. The right to be heard.

When the briefing ended, engines were already idling, their deep rumble filling the lot. Drivers moved back toward their rigs, shaking hands and calling out goodbyes to volunteers. The air smelled of diesel and anticipation. I climbed back into my truck, set my coffee in the holder, and turned the key. The familiar vibration settled through the cab—a sound that felt like purpose.

We filed out slowly, one lane at a time, looping around to the Go-Mart across the road to fuel up. Each rig pulled through, filled its tanks, and rolled back into position. The convoy was a well-oiled machine now. By the time the last rig had fueled, the radio came alive again.

"All right, Convoy," came the call. "Let's roll east."

And with that, we did.

The road ahead wound through Ohio, then Pennsylvania. We took the toll roads, the line of trucks stretching for miles, each one marked by flags snapping in the wind. The landscape began to change—rolling hills, bare winter trees, and the faint haze of distant mountains. The radios crackled with chatter and laughter, but underneath it all, there was a quiet hum of nerves. This was the final stretch.

Stefan from One America News joined me for that last leg of the journey. He wanted to see the arrival firsthand, to capture the moment we reached Hagerstown. I could tell he was as excited as I was.

As we crossed into Maryland, the traffic on the overpasses thickened. People waved flags, cheered, and flashed headlights as we passed beneath. Every mile closer, the crowds grew larger. The CB radio was alive with emotion—drivers shouting their disbelief, their gratitude, their pride.

Then, as we turned onto the final stretch of road leading toward Hagerstown Speedway, the scene ahead took my breath away. Both of us rolled our windows down.

Both sides of the road were lined with people. Yards were packed shoulder to shoulder, flags of every size whipping in the cold March wind. Families waved handmade signs, veterans stood at attention, kids sat on their parents' shoulders shouting, "Welcome home!" The sound of horns filled the air—deep, rolling, unrelenting. You couldn't hear yourself think over it, and it didn't matter.

At the entrance to the speedway, a massive rotator tow truck stood parked, its crane arm extended high into the air, holding a giant American flag that rippled proudly in the wind. Stefan leaned over and hit the horn again and again, his grin stretching from ear to ear. Every blast echoed off the crowd, a rolling wave of sound that seemed to shake the ground beneath us.

Inside, the lot was already crowded with other convoys—groups that had come up from Florida, from the North, from all corners of the country. They had been waiting for us, and as we rolled in, they greeted us like brothers coming home. The energy was electric. People shouted, waved, hugged strangers, and cried.

Volunteers directed us into the maze of parking lanes. We moved slowly, carefully, snaking around the curves of the speedway grounds. When I finally found my spot, I set the brakes and sat there for a long moment, just taking it in. The roar of engines, the shouts, the music—it was overwhelming.

I looked over at Stefan. He was quiet now, the camera in his lap, his eyes glistening. "That was incredible," he said softly. Then he shook my hand. "We made it."

I smiled. "Yeah," I said. "We did."

He climbed down from the cab, his camera gear slung over his shoulder, and disappeared into the growing crowd. I stayed a while longer, just breathing it in. The sense of completion. Of arrival. But also, of something beginning.

All around, volunteers were already at work. Trucks full of donated supplies backed up to the unloading area—pallets of bottled water, food, clothing, hygiene items—all being sorted beneath the speedway bleachers by teams of volunteers. The organization was impressive.

Lines of porta-potties and portable shower trailers had been set up as well. The place had become a temporary city.

Mike Landis parked his rig near the main stadium entrance, his truck positioned behind a flatbed that would serve as the main stage. One by one, the last of the trucks rolled in, and when the final engine shut down, every inch of that speedway lot was full. The sound of air brakes echoed like a final exhale.

As dusk fell, the floodlights came on, bathing the area in gold. People gathered near the stage, music playing softly from nearby speakers. Someone lit a bonfire, then another. The smell of wood smoke and diesel hung in the air. Laughter mixed with quiet conversation. A sense of peace settled over the grounds.

When the evening rally began, we stood shoulder to shoulder once more. Brian spoke briefly—thanking everyone, reminding us why we were there. Then came the evening prayer. When the final "Amen" was spoken, music filled the air again, and the night belonged to the people.

I walked the perimeter for a while, watching the glow of the fires, the flags still waving in the dark, the faces lit by pride and exhaustion. I didn't know what tomorrow would bring. None of us did. But I knew this much: we'd kept our promise. We'd made it.

I returned to my truck, climbed inside, and sat for a long moment before closing the curtain. The air was cool, the noise of the camp fading to a steady hum. My heart was full.

We had come from the deserts of California to the far hills of Maryland. We had carried the voices of a nation. And now, on the edge of Washington, D.C., we were finally here.

Tomorrow, the real test would begin.

Chapter 16 – Seventy Miles to Washington

The first morning in Hagerstown broke cold and quiet. The sun was just a pale streak behind the horizon, barely touching the frost that clung to the trucks and the steel guardrails around the track. I cracked open my cab door, and the smell of diesel and woodsmoke rolled in. Somewhere nearby, someone was frying bacon on a camp stove. The low murmur of idling engines blended with quiet conversation as drivers began to stir for the day.

We had made it—seventy miles from Washington, D.C.
Close enough to taste the victory, but far enough to feel the weight of what still lay ahead.

Near the parking-lot side of the grandstands, a group of Christian volunteers had already set up two folding tables under a small canopy with donuts and coffee. I followed the smell like a compass and stood among other early risers, our breath clouding in the cold. The coffee was strong and a little burnt, but it felt like warmth in a cup. Someone said grace before we ate, and a few of us bowed our heads. That first sip of coffee that morning felt like a reminder: **we weren't done yet.**

By eight o'clock, the camp had come alive. Vendors opened small stands selling flags and T-shirts. Drivers stood in groups, hands shoved into pockets, talking about what came next. It felt like a strange mix of a county fair and a deployment camp. Everyone was proud—but restless. We had made it across the country, but the mission still felt incomplete.

Brian, Mike, and Marcus climbed onto the flatbed stage near the grandstands. A crowd formed—hundreds of us bundled in coats and gloves, facing the makeshift podium as the speakers crackled to life. The Pledge of Allegiance came first, then a prayer, and finally Brian took the microphone.

He spoke about patience. About strategy.
He told us D.C. wasn't letting the convoy enter the city. Every highway exit that led toward the capital was blocked by police cruisers and heavy equipment—snowplows, dump trucks, and barricades. The plan now was to "run the loop," circling the Beltway as one long, rolling reminder that the people were still watching.

It wasn't what many wanted to hear. You could feel the shift in the crowd—the frustration, the letdown. Some had imagined rolling into the heart of the capital, horns blaring, flags flying. But that wasn't the fight we were walking into. This was a test of endurance, not confrontation.

When the morning rally ended, some climbed back into their trucks, ready to run the loop. Others, like me, stayed behind. There was work to do.

I spent that day helping reorganize the parking layout. Trucks had been parked haphazardly after our arrival, and if one needed to move, a dozen others had to shift first. So we set up a plan. A few of us formed a crew and directed rigs into cleaner rows. It reminded me of my Air Force days—FOD walks and precision.

After the lot was clear, I helped run the forklift, moving pallets of donations into place under the bleachers. Boxes of bottled water were stacked six feet high beside crates of canned goods, hygiene kits, and winter clothes. People from all across the country had sent what they could.

That afternoon, the sun finally broke through the clouds, and the mood in camp began to lift. Someone was grilling hot dogs near the main gate, and kids were handing out hand-drawn thank-you cards to drivers. I paused long enough to eat, sitting on a trailer step, thinking how this felt less like a protest and more like a living town—built from faith, grit, and purpose.

As the trucks rolled back in that evening from their Beltway run, the convoy lights flickered like a river of fire across the horizon. Horns echoed faintly from the highway as the last few rigs pulled back into the speedway. The mood was calmer now—some disappointed, some proud —but everyone still united. We were seventy miles from the capital, holding the line, waiting for the next move.

That night, I joined a few of the organizers and supporters inside one of the larger coaches—a warm refuge from the cold wind sweeping across the track. The meeting inside was half strategy, half exhaustion. The conversation turned toward Washington—how to reach those who could make change, how to turn the noise of the convoy into a voice that mattered.

In the days that followed, I sometimes joined the runs around the Beltway. Other days, I stayed back to help at the speedway. One afternoon, while walking the grounds and talking with drivers, I spotted a familiar face outside Jeff's coach—it was **Ann Vandersteel**, from *Steel Truth*.

I remember asking, "Are you Ann Vandersteel?" She smiled. She was wearing a red, white, and blue leather jacket patterned like the American flag.

"I am," she said.

"I've followed you for a long time," I told her. After a few minutes of conversation, I realized she'd been following me too—on my Telegram channel. Small world.

She introduced me to her producer, Elizabeth, who was parked out by the highway near the main gate. Together, we conducted an interview with Laura-Lynn Tyler Thompson—former co-host of *700 Club Canada* and now an independent journalist producing news segments on Facebook. We wrapped up the interview and later decided to grab dinner together at a nearby restaurant.

As we sat down, a man from the convoy—clearly frustrated—recognized Ann and approached our table. His voice was raised, angry about what he believed the organizers were or weren't doing. He accused Ann of knowing more than she was sharing and demanded answers. His tone grew sharp enough to draw the attention of the restaurant staff, who soon came over, ready to ask him to leave.

I motioned for them to hold on a moment.
"Brother," I said, "I understand how you feel. We all came across this country because we wanted change—but storming Washington isn't the answer. Give it a day. Breathe. I promise you, in twenty-four hours, you'll see where this is going."

He paused, then nodded. The tension eased, and he left quietly. Across the table, Ann watched in silence. Elizabeth, sitting beside me, had quietly recorded the entire exchange. Later, she would release it as part of a *Steel Truth* episode.

That night, back at the coach, I sat quietly while others spoke. Then Jeff—the same man I'd first met in Adelanto—looked up from his phone.

"Ron," he said, "would you be interested in joining the group that's going to D.C. tomorrow? There's a meeting with senators. Brian and a few others are going. I think you should be there."

For a moment, I didn't speak. My mind flashed back to the thousands of faces along the bridges—the notes and prayers tucked into paper bags, the people who had grabbed my hand and said, *'Tell them for us.'*

I looked at Jeff and said, "Yes. I'd be honored."

That night, I laid in my sleeper staring up at the ceiling, the hum of nearby generators breaking the silence. Outside, the flags rustled softly in the wind. I thought about how far we'd come—from the desert of Adelanto to the farmlands of Indiana, through snow, rain, and endless miles of open road.

We were here now—**seventy miles from Washington.**
The fight had changed, but the mission hadn't.
Tomorrow, I wouldn't be driving a truck—
I'd be carrying the voices of the people.

As dawn approached, the sky over Hagerstown turned the color of steel. The air bit cold against my face as I stepped out of my cab, coffee in hand, watching my breath drift into the dim light. The organizer's bus sat parked beside my truck, its engine rumbling low, exhaust curling like smoke signals into the morning air. Inside, Brian, and a few others were already aboard—faces set with quiet determination.

I climbed the steps, the sound of my boots on metal echoing faintly in the stillness. As I took my seat, it struck me that this would be the first time since leaving California that I wouldn't be behind the wheel of my truck. Today, I wasn't a driver—I was a messenger. The promises I'd made along the way—the handshakes, the words, the prayers—were all coming with me.

We were seventy miles from Washington, and now we were going to carry the people's voice to its doorstep.

Chapter 17 – Carrying the People's Voice

The ride into Washington was quiet at first. Morning light spilled silver across the Maryland fields as our bus rolled toward D.C. There were six of us onboard — Brian, the convoy's press liaison Lisa, a few drivers who'd worked with Brian in earlier movements, and a young man from California we all called *Kid Cowboy* — Jauneil Brooks.

He was only eighteen or nineteen, but he carried himself like a seasoned hand at rallies — always in boots, a wide-brimmed hat, and a belt buckle big enough to catch the sunrise.

The air inside the bus was thick with tension and purpose. Phones buzzed as political consultants went over what to say — and what *not* to say — when we met the senators. But we already knew what we were going to do. We weren't there to act like politicians or tailor our words to please anyone. We were going to be ourselves — straightforward, honest, and unapologetically American.

When we reached Capitol Hill, the bus dropped us off a few blocks away. The streets were quiet and cold, the sound of traffic echoing off the marble buildings. We walked the rest of the way, our breath visible in the morning air, boots striking against the concrete sidewalk.

At the security checkpoint, we paused and waited for Dr. Paul Alexander and Dr. Pierre Kory to arrive. They had traveled separately but would join us for the meetings that morning. Their presence added weight to what was already a significant day — science, medicine, and the voices of everyday Americans all converging under the same cause.

After clearing security, the senators' staffers met us and escorted the group toward the Capitol complex. We descended into the tunnels connecting the Senate offices to the main building, boarding the small underground subway that ferried staff and members between chambers. As the car hummed along the tracks, I remember thinking how surreal it was — rolling through the heart of the nation's government with the voices of the people still echoing in my head from every bridge and roadside across America.

The day before, Brian had made something clear: if our livestreamer wasn't allowed into the meetings, we wouldn't hold them. "Transparency or nothing," he'd said. To their credit, the senators agreed. Cameras would roll from start to finish.

We were ushered into a formal conference room. Senators Ted Cruz and Ron Johnson entered shortly after and greeted us warmly. There was no fanfare, no speeches — just a handshake and a nod to begin.

Left to right: Senators Ted Cruz, Ron Johnson, Dr. Paul Alexander, and Ron "Grey Wolf" Coleman

One by one, we spoke — Brian leading the way. We told them what we'd seen across the country: the crowds on the overpasses, the flags waving in the wind, the people standing in the cold — some smiling, some crying — holding signs that read, *"They work for us."*

When my turn came, I spoke of the promises I'd made — to carry those voices to Washington, to deliver the messages written in shaky handwriting on brown paper bags and tucked into truck doors by people who believed they had been forgotten.

I shared one of those notes:

"Dear Trucker, I admire your courage and determination in doing this. I will support you in prayer for a victory over the sad oppression that is going on. Thank you for fighting for us all.— A mother of three. God bless."

For a moment, the room fell silent. I let the words hang there before I continued.

I spoke about what had driven me — what had driven all of us. That the America we loved was still there, buried beneath fear and bureaucracy, waiting for her people to stand again. That the reach of government had grown too long, too powerful, too detached from the governed. We weren't there for attention or recognition. We were there to remind them of their oath — to the Constitution and to the people it protects.

For more than two hours, the senators listened. They didn't rush us. They asked questions, took notes, and spoke candidly about their own frustrations. Both Senator Cruz and Senator Johnson had already supported efforts to end the national emergency declarations, but they admitted it was an uphill fight. The administration had vowed to veto any attempt to limit executive power, and the House majority had no intention of letting such legislation reach the floor.

Still, there was a shared sense of understanding in that room — a recognition that something fundamental had shifted in the country, that the people were no longer silent.

I ended my turn with a simple, resolute statement:

"Let Nancy Pelosi know that the power is in the people — and we are coming."

Senator Cruz nodded, his expression firm, eyes steady. *"Amen,"* he said quietly.

When the meeting ended, we shook hands and left for lunch before our next appointment — this time with members of the House of Representatives. We had requested that both Republicans and Democrats attend, because this wasn't about party lines. It was about America.

When we arrived for the two p.m. meeting, only five Republican members were there. No Democrats showed. At first, the House staff refused to allow our livestreamer inside, but Brian stood firm. "We don't do closed doors," he said. After a tense pause, they relented, and the cameras were set up.

The tone was different from the Senate. The congressmen seemed distracted, their body language stiff. One of them, seated at the head of the table, leaned back and said bluntly, "There's not much we can do right now. We're not in the majority."

That hit a nerve. I leaned forward and asked, "So you're saying that after everything we've done — all the miles, all the people who waved from bridges — you're telling me we'd have to bring every one of them here, to Washington, just to be heard?"

He looked at me and shrugged. "Yes."

The room went still. There wasn't anything more to say. We'd come all this way to deliver the people's voice — and they'd just confirmed what many already feared.

We left quietly. Outside, the city buzzed with traffic and the steady hum of everyday life, but for a while, none of us spoke. The weight of what we'd just done lingered in the silence between us.

We stopped in front of the Capitol steps, taking a few photos together — a small group of ordinary Americans who had come to deliver the voices of millions. Then we walked until we found a small restaurant tucked off a side street, sat down, and shared a meal.

There was some disappointment, yes — but also a deep sense of fulfillment. We had done what we came to do. We had carried the message, spoken the truth, and kept our promise to the people who believed in us.

For the first time in weeks, the noise inside me quieted. We had fulfilled our purpose.

That evening, the bus rolled back north, headlights cutting through the darkness on the seventy-mile stretch to Hagerstown. When we pulled into the speedway, the camp was alive with bonfires, music, horns blaring and cheers. People crowded around, shaking our hands, thanking us for representing them.

For me, that night marked something more than the end of a mission — it was the fulfillment of a promise. I had carried their words into the heart of Washington and spoken them aloud.

As the camp quieted and the fires burned low, I sat in my truck, looking toward the faint glow on the horizon — the direction of Washington. We'd carried the people's voice to the very heart of power, but something deeper had begun to stir. This was no longer just a convoy; it was a calling. The road ahead would test not just our engines, but our spirit — and for me, the journey to make America great again was only beginning.

Chapter 18 – The Road Beyond the Capitol

When we rolled back into Hagerstown after the meetings in Washington, the air felt different.

Part victory, part exhaustion. We had done what we said we would do — carry the people's voice straight into the halls of power — and we'd done it with integrity. For some, that was enough. For others, it wasn't even close.

As we pulled into the speedway, horns blared, campfires glowed, and people crowded around to welcome us back. They shook our hands, hugged us, thanked us for standing up for them. Yet behind every smile, I could feel a question hanging in the air: Now what?

***

The Echo After the Applause

In the days that followed, that question became the camp's heartbeat. Some believed we had achieved our purpose. We said we'd take the people's message to D.C., and we had. Others felt the fight had only begun — that we should roll into the capital itself, park our rigs on Constitution Avenue, and make them listen by staying put.

I listened to every side. Part of me understood the frustration. But deep down, I knew occupation wasn't the answer. We'd been heard; whether they acted or not was on them now.

I stuck around Hagerstown while others left for home. Something in me said the work wasn't finished yet — just changing shape. Every movement reaches that moment when the adrenaline fades, and what's left is purpose. You find out who's in it for the cameras and who's in it for the cause.

A few days later, that purpose showed up in the form of a familiar face.

***

A Visit from Senator Cruz

When word spread that Senator Ted Cruz was coming to Hagerstown, the energy shifted again. He took the stage that morning, his voice carrying over the crowd and the steady hum of idling trucks. He thanked us for what we'd done — for representing millions who felt forgotten. He told us to hold the line, to keep standing for freedom.

After Senator Cruz finished speaking, he stepped down from the stage to meet with Brian Brase and Mike Landis. The three talked briefly before Cruz followed Mike to his truck. He was going to ride back to Washington, D.C., fulfilling a promise Mike had made to the daughter of a World War II veteran — to carry her father's 48-star flag all the way to the heart of the nation's capital.

As Mike climbed into the driver's seat and warmed up the engine, Senator Cruz took the passenger side, the door still open as people gathered around to watch. I walked up, stepped onto the running board, and leaned in beside him. We snapped a quick selfie — two men on very different roads but sharing the same purpose.

Senator Ted Cruz and Ron "Grey Wolf" Coleman, Hagerstown, MD. — March 2022

Then he turned toward me, his expression firm and his voice low enough that only I could hear.

94

"Ron," he said, "don't give up what you're doing. You're on the right side of things here. Don't stop."

We shook hands.

"I won't," I told him.

His words followed me long after he drove away, echoing across the lot that night and into the silence of the desert miles ahead. At first they felt like encouragement, but the longer I turned them over in my mind, the more they sounded like a command. I didn't know what form it would take yet — only that the road wasn't finished with me.

Even though we'd just come from meeting him in D.C., hearing those words again — there on the ground, surrounded by dust, diesel, and ordinary Americans — felt different. It wasn't politics; it was conviction.

As Mike pulled away with Senator Cruz on board, I made my way back through the crowd. A few voices behind me said, "It was all just a gimmick."

I stopped and turned toward them.

"You're wrong," I said.

They looked at me, waiting.

"Because his visit — his standing here, on this ground, with us — gave this convoy something real: legitimacy. A sitting United States senator just put his name and face on what we're doing. That means something."

***

The Fracture in the Ranks

Still, cracks were showing. Some drivers packed up, feeling their mission was done. Others muttered that we hadn't gone far enough. There were heated discussions around campfires and over the CB.

Some pushed for direct action — rolling into the city despite the blocked exits, forcing the issue. A few tried. One driver was ticketed and had his truck towed. It was clear the authorities were done tolerating the spectacle.

For me though, something deeper was happening. I began to realize that maybe the battle wasn't just in Washington — maybe it was in understanding why so many Americans had stopped believing they had a voice at all.

So while others argued tactics, I started talking — to anyone who'd listen.

***

From Driver to Teacher

I'd always been comfortable behind a wheel or a wrench, but standing in front of a crowd was something new. Yet as I walked around the speedway, talking with people, small groups started forming around me. They asked questions — about the Constitution, about their rights, about how the government was supposed to work.

That's when I started livestreaming.

I set up my phone and began holding what I called "Constitutional Conversations." Sometimes I streamed them while parked; other times, I spoke as I drove. I talked about the differences between federal and state powers, about what the words on the parchment truly meant, and how the structure of the three branches reflected those first three articles — Article I creating the legislative, Article II the executive, and Article III the judicial. I'd explain that the Constitution wasn't just a document; it was a blueprint.

During those days at the speedway, people began following regularly. Some were fellow drivers, others veterans, families sitting together at home, or just curious Americans trying to make sense of a country that suddenly felt unfamiliar. The chats filled with questions, stories, and gratitude. It was no longer just commentary — it was connection.

One of those listeners was a woman who reached out to my daughter — who was moderating for me — during one of my livestreams. She volunteered to help, offering to take on some of the work as a moderator. By then, I had close to a dozen moderators, and she quickly became one of the most dependable — keeping the comments civil, organizing information, and helping new people find their way into the conversation.

It wasn't until much later that I learned how much those livestreams had meant to her. She told me she'd never paid much attention to politics before — it had always felt distant, like something happening somewhere else. But after listening to my talks about the Constitution, she said she'd learned things she'd never known.

"You made it real," she said. "And now I see that your journey is really our journey too."

Her words stayed with me. They reminded me that what we were doing wasn't just about protest — it was about education, awakening, and reconnection. We were rebuilding something that had been lost: civic understanding, shared purpose, and belief in the Constitution itself.

It amazed me how many people had never been taught those things. Not because they didn't care — but because no one had ever shown them.

I thought back to Monrovia, weeks earlier, when I'd spoken to teenagers about civic responsibility. This was the same thing, only larger. I wasn't a politician or a professor — just a man trying to remind people how their country actually worked.

Before long, those livestreams became a kind of rolling classroom — a place where people could ask questions, challenge ideas, and rediscover what it meant to be American. And that's when it hit me: I wasn't alone on this road.

For the first time, I realized the movement had grown far beyond the trucks and rallies. It had become something personal — a shared journey toward truth and renewal. And as the weeks went on, a thought began to take shape in my mind: if people could find hope and understanding through a screen, what might happen if I carried that message farther — on foot, across the country itself?

That was the seed of what would come next — the *Grey Wolf Walk Across America for Freedom.*

***

A Movement in the Making

Over those weeks in Hagerstown, I saw something beautiful happen. Strangers became friends. People who'd arrived angry left inspired. We weren't just driving freight anymore — we were hauling truth.

When Dr. Robert Malone came out to speak near the end of our first stay, it added another layer. Here was a man who'd helped develop the very technology behind the vaccines — standing in front of us, warning about censorship, corruption, and the loss of medical freedom.

The crowd listened in silence. His presence validated what many already felt: that this movement wasn't fringe, it was American — a collective demand for honesty.

Still, even with the speakers and rallies, the question kept resurfacing in my mind: What now?

***

Back on the Road

The organizers knew the energy was fading—you could hear it in their voices, see it on their faces—. Repetition was killing momentum. Driving loops around the Beltway was making a point, but it wasn't moving hearts anymore.

Then one evening, Mike Landis took to the stage. "We're heading back to California," he announced. "We've got ten state bills out there that attack moral and medical freedom — and we're going to bring attention to every one of them."

The crowd roared. The loudest reaction came when he mentioned one of those bills — a proposal that would have allowed the termination of a baby's life, weeks after birth. It was beyond comprehension.

So the convoy packed up and rolled west.

The trip felt different this time — less about confrontation, more about carrying the flame home. We stopped in towns along the way, meeting people who waved flags and handed us food. By the time we reached Sacramento, we were tired but resolute.

We stayed at a raceway outside the city, circling and occupying the capitol a few times before the convoy began to splinter again. Some were heading home, others were planning the next phase.

Mike Landis and I both knew it was time to step back for a bit. We each had bills to pay and families to support. He returned to work, and I followed — hauling his friend's trailer back to Pennsylvania. Mike helped me line up a job hauling bulk sugar to keep things steady for a while. I planned to rejoin once the convoy regrouped in Hagerstown for the second time.

But somewhere along those long stretches of interstate, I began to feel something shift — quiet at first, like the hum beneath the tires, but growing with every mile.

***

The Quiet Realization

As I drove across the plains, I replayed Senator Cruz's words in my mind: Don't give up what you're doing.

At first, I'd thought he meant the convoy. But now, I began to think he meant something larger.

The convoy had accomplished what it could. We'd made noise, built community, and carried the message to Washington. But change wasn't going to come from sheer horsepower. It had to come from endurance — from persistence of spirit.

And that's when the idea began to take shape.

***

The Teacher Becomes the Walker

When I made it back to Pennsylvania, the convoy had already pushed on toward the Pacific Northwest — a zigzag route meant to draw attention across the states before returning to Hagerstown. But plans changed. After a brief stop in Washington State, the convoy made a straight shot back east.

Something about it didn't sit right with me anymore. The mission felt scattered. The message was blurring. The voices at the rallies were starting to sound less like resolve and more like anger — less about freedom, more about revenge.

It was time to find my own path.

One evening, sitting in my truck outside a small truck stop in Pennsylvania, I thought about what truly mattered — what still needed to change. Three things stood out, clear as the sunset:

1. End the State of Emergency.

It had been used and abused to justify restrictions on freedom, to shut down livelihoods, and to consolidate power.

2. Reform the National Emergencies Act.

No government should ever again have the authority to hold its people hostage under open-ended decrees.

3. Hold accountable those who abused that power.

Liberty means nothing if tyranny carries no consequence.

Those would be my objectives. Not a list of a hundred grievances — just three core truths worth walking for.

The idea sounded impossible. I was sixty-two years old. But impossible didn't mean wrong.

So I prayed on it, and consulted with friends and family. I reflected on everything I'd seen over those eighty-seven days — the faces, the flags, the miles. And I realized that the convoy had given me more than a platform. It had given me a purpose.

The trucks had carried the voice of the people to the steps of power. Now, maybe it was time for one man to carry it further — not on wheels, but on foot.

***

The Next Call to the Road

When the convoy returned to Hagerstown that May, I went to meet them. I could tell right away things weren't the same. The fire had dimmed. The mission had scattered into side projects and arguments over leadership. That was when the original remaining organizers agreed to bring the convoy to an end.

So I stepped back, the movement was bigger than any one name or event now.

I thought about how every great American stand — from Lexington to Selma — had required ordinary people to do extraordinary things, often alone. Maybe that was what was next for me.

That night, as I watched the campfires flicker and heard the low murmur of engines idling in the distance, the thought became conviction.

The convoy had rolled.
Now I would walk.

Chapter 19 – The Call to Walk

The final evening in Hagerstown was heavy with tension. Campfires burned low, voices were raised in frustration, and even the hum of idling trucks felt uncertain. Some drivers wanted to roll into D.C. and occupy the streets, convinced that parking their rigs on Constitution Avenue would force change. Others, quieter but no less passionate, believed our mission was done.

I stood in the middle of it all, listening. The anger was real — I felt it too — but I couldn't justify a move that I knew would bear no fruit. We'd taken the people's voice to Washington; that was what we'd promised, and we'd kept that promise. I tried to tell the men and women gathered around that day that occupying the capital wouldn't move the needle. It would undo everything we'd earned — the trust, the legitimacy, the message of unity.

Still, there was heartbreak as people began packing up. Hugs, handshakes, final photos. The convoy had become a family, and like any family, parting hurt.

That evening, I climbed into my truck and pointed north. Back to Pennsylvania. Back to work.

***

Back Behind the Wheel

I picked up hauling bulk sugar out of Pennsylvania — honest work, steady pay. The kind that let me keep moving while I sorted out what came next. The road has a way of clearing your thoughts, and mile after mile, I found myself replaying everything that had happened since Adelanto: the bridges filled with waving flags, the supporters, the meetings in D.C., and the look on Senator Cruz's face when he'd told me not to stop.

Don't stop.

Those two words started to echo louder than my engine.

At night, parked at a small truck stop in Pennsylvania, I'd sit with my laptop open, my map book spread across the table, a cup of coffee cooling beside me. Something was forming in my mind — something different. The convoy had carried a message on eighteen wheels. Maybe it was time to carry it another way.

***

The First Sketches of a Walk

At first it sounded crazy, even to me. Walk across America? At sixty-two? But the more I thought about it, the more it made sense.

Walking was pure. Honest. No noise, no filters, no engines. Just one man, one flag, and one message: liberty.

I began mapping potential routes — highways that allowed foot travel, distances between towns, elevation gains. I kept coming back to U.S. 50, known as The Loneliest Road in America. It stretched from California to the East Coast, slicing through the very heart of the country. That loneliness was exactly what I wanted — quiet enough to think, to talk, and to meet Americans face-to-face.

Between sugar loads, I fine-tuned the plan. I'd start in Carson City, Nevada — my home state's capital — and walk east to Washington D.C. I'd livestream as much as possible, using the same online network that had grown during the convoy. My moderators, now close friends, offered to help with logistics: rally stops, sheriff introductions through CSPOA, and online updates.

Bit by bit, the impossible began to look inevitable.

***

The Road Home

When my last Pennsylvania run ended, I fired up the Kenworth and started west. Glory, my big U.S. flag, flew from a pole on the rear of the truck, snapping in the wind. I wasn't hauling freight this time — just purpose.

I stopped again in Hagerstown to see a few friends still camped near the track. We shook hands, hugged, wished each other luck, and talked about the road ahead. Some were still chasing convoys, but for me, the route was set.

Crossing the plains, I started scouting sections of the walk in reverse — noting shoulders wide enough for safety, towns with motels or cafés, and potential rally points. Colorado's peaks loomed in the distance, then gave way to Utah's red canyons and finally the vast desert stretch of Nevada.

That drive confirmed what I already knew: this would be the hardest thing I'd ever do. But it also felt right — as if every mile of the convoy had been leading to this one decision.

***

Preparation in Reno

By the time I rolled into Reno, I was all in. I parked the truck and turned my attention to the old 1967 motorhome sitting beside my house —tired, faded, but full of possibility. I called it my chase rig, nicknamed *Beechy*, the support vehicle that would follow me across the country.

That's when my neighbor, Bubba, stepped in to help. Bubba was a big man with a bigger heart—always ready with a joke, a story, or a wrench. He offered to be my driver during the walk, keeping *Beechy* close behind and handling supplies and safety. For days we worked side by side beneath that doghouse engine cover, swapping parts, rewiring lights, installing a swamp cooler, and laughing about how the old rig probably hadn't seen this much attention since Nixon was in office.

For a while, everything felt like it was coming together.

***

A Sudden Loss

Then, one morning in late June, I came home from the hardware store and saw him—slumped backward across the engine compartment, motionless.

Bubba was gone.

The coroner said it was sudden, likely a heart issue—nothing anyone could have seen coming. He was only in his early forties.

Neighbors gathered. Friends came by to offer comfort. Some said I should postpone the walk, take time to grieve, to regroup. But deep down, I knew what Bubba would have told me: Keep going, brother. Don't stop now.

So that's what I decided to do. Even if I had to haul my gear in a wagon and sleep in a tent on the side of the highway, I would walk.

That conviction became steel in my spine.

***

The Arrival of Mr. T

A short time later, I mentioned on a livestream that I'd need a new driver. One supporter said she might know someone willing to help. Soon after, I got a call from a man I'd met during the second half of the convoy—a solid, quiet type we would eventually call Mr. T.

He'd heard about Bubba's passing and didn't hesitate.

"I'll drive for you," he said simply. "I'll be there tomorrow."

He left his home in Kansas that evening and drove straight through, stopping only for naps at rest areas. By the next afternoon, his pickup rolled into Reno. We stood in my driveway, shook hands, and started finishing what Bubba and I had begun—checking brakes, lights, fluids, and loading supplies.

For the first time since Hagerstown, I felt peace again. The road was calling, and now I had a partner to help answer.

The plan was simple: spend the last days of June finishing the motorhome and testing the equipment, then drive to Carson City on the morning of July 2.

That day, the walk would begin.

The *Grey Wolf Walk Across America for Freedom* finally had a heartbeat.

Chapter 20 – The Night Before the Walk

The evening of July 1 settled soft and golden over Sun Valley, Nevada. The air smelled of dust and sagebrush — that faint desert perfume you only notice when the wind stills long enough for memory to rise with it. From the front yard I could see the mountains etched in amber light, their edges fading into the darkening blue. The hum of *Beechy's* generator being tested mixed with the song of crickets and the low whine of a cooling engine.

Beechy, my old 1967 motorhome — patched, weathered, but proud — sat in the driveway gleaming in the fading light like an old warhorse ready for one last campaign. Inside, the final pieces were coming together. My daughter and grandson were scrambling to help pack supplies, working with Mr. T to fit everything inside: donated drinks, snacks, food, first-aid supplies — the kindness of strangers turned into survival gear.

My neighbor wandered over to wish us well. He leaned on his fence and called out, "You really walking all the way to D.C.?"

I smiled. "That's the plan."

He shook his head, half in disbelief, half in admiration. "Well, if anyone's stubborn enough to do it, it's you."

The smell of fuel and sun-baked metal filled the yard. My grandson packed boxes with donations, while my daughter double-checked lists and labeled them. The ordinary sounds of family — laughter, footsteps, the squeak of a cooler lid — felt sacred that night.

***

Reflections and Resolve

I sat in *Beechy's* small kitchenette while the evening deepened outside. Through the window I could see the distant glow of Reno, quiet and still, except for the faint clatter of tools as Mr. T worked nearby. The desert light faded to purple, and I found myself staring at my reflection in the window — a man lined by miles, by worry, but still standing.

I thought about everything that had brought me here — the long highways, the convoy, the bridges lined with waving flags and faces,

Bubba's laughter echoing in the yard, and the steady conviction that had carried me since Senator Cruz's words: Don't give up what you're doing.

The convoy had been about unity.

The walk would be about endurance.

It was no longer about diesel engines or radio chatter. It was about the slow rhythm of footsteps and the persistence of faith. I thought about what freedom really meant — not the slogans or the speeches, but the quiet right to choose one's path and speak one's truth without fear. That's what I was walking for.

My moderators were already coordinating schedules, social-media posts, contact lists for sheriffs along the route, and nightly stopping points. They'd become more than volunteers; they were a remote support crew, a digital family watching from all around the country.

CSPOA founder Richard Mack had offered encouragement, telling me, "You'll meet the real America out there." I believed him. Out there, beyond the headlines, I knew I'd find people who still believed in what this nation was supposed to be.

Still, a quiet fear lingered — not of the miles, but of the unknown. Could one man really carry a message that far? Could he make people listen?

I bowed my head and whispered a prayer.

"Lord, if this is Your will, then give me the strength to see it through."

***

Final Preparations

Mr. T came over, wiping his hands on a rag. "Everything's ready," he said. "We roll in the morning."

We walked around *Beechy* one last time. The new lettering gleamed under the porch light — banners sent by supporters that we'd carefully fastened on the back:

CAUTION — WALKERS FOR FREEDOM AHEAD.

He grinned. "Looks official now."

I smiled back. "It's as official as it needs to be."

The banner fluttered slightly in the night breeze, and for a moment I felt the weight of it — not fabric, but expectation.

Inside the house, I laid my walking clothes and sneakers at the end of my bed. My daughter hugged me tight. "Dad, just promise me you'll be careful," she said.

"I will," I told her, though we both knew there was no guarantee.

Before turning in, I sent a short message to my online followers:

Tomorrow, I take the first step of the Grey Wolf Walk Across America for Freedom — from the steps of the Nevada State Capitol to the steps of our nation's Capitol. For liberty. For truth. For every American who still believes this country can stand tall again.

The replies started pouring in — words of support, prayers, emojis, flags. Some came from truckers I'd met on the road; others from strangers who'd followed since the convoy. It reminded me that I wasn't walking alone.

***

The Quiet Before Dawn

Mr. T, my daughter, and my grandson worked late into the night, packing the last boxes into *Beechy*. The sounds of their voices drifted through the window as I sat for a moment longer, letting the weight of it all settle in.

I knew I needed sleep — it was approaching midnight — but every creak of the house sounded louder than usual. I wasn't nervous; I was simply aware. Aware that tomorrow, everything would change.

Before going to bed, I stepped outside. The desert sky stretched endless and black, stars burning bright above the silhouette of Peavine Mountain to the west. A warm wind brushed past, carrying the faint scent of sage and distant asphalt. I could almost trace the road in my mind — Carson City, Fallon, Ely, and beyond — across mountains, plains, and heartland towns that still believed in freedom.

A porch light flickered somewhere down the street. The neighborhood slept, unaware that in a few hours, a 62-year-old man would begin a walk across the continent, armed with nothing more than faith and a message.

I closed my eyes and breathed in the silence.

Tomorrow, I would walk.

Not for fame. Not for politics.

But because somewhere along the road between Adelanto and Washington — between diesel smoke and prayer — I had rediscovered what it meant to be American.

As the last lights in the house flickered out, I could still hear the low hum of *Beechy's* generator and the desert wind brushing against the siding. Sleep came in fragments. When dawn finally broke, the first pale light spilled across the mountains and caught the side of the motorhome. Mr. T was already outside, sipping coffee, the banner fluttering behind him. I stepped onto the porch, heart steady.

It was time to walk.

Chapter 21 – The First Steps

The morning of July 2, 2022, broke warm and pale over Sun Valley, Nevada. Mr. T and I gave long hugs to my daughter and grandson before climbing aboard *Beechy*, my old 1967 motorhome. She groaned awake like an old friend answering one more call to the open road. Abby—my four-legged shadow and unofficial mascot—hopped up in her seat, ears straight up as usual.

Mr. T was still new to the area and didn't want to navigate Reno traffic, so he asked me to take the wheel.

"I'll watch and learn her quirks," he said, securing his seat belt.

It had been years since *Beechy* had touched the highway. The sound of her engine rising through the gears brought back every road I'd ever known with her. As we rolled south toward Carson City, the same current of purpose hummed through me again—a mix of faith, anticipation, and the quiet question that always comes before something greater begins: *Will anyone join me this time?*

***

No Crowd, No Fanfare

We arrived early at the Nevada State Capitol. The dome gleamed under the sharp morning sun. I checked the live-stream setup while Mr. T positioned *Beechy* near the curb, the *"Walk for Freedom"* banner fluttering in the light breeze.

I'd told my online supporters I'd be starting at eight sharp. In my heart, I hoped a few locals might appear—someone to walk that first mile beside me. But no one came. No crowd. No press. No cheers.

For a moment, the silence cut deep. Starting alone weighed heavier than I'd expected. I thought of what someone had told me back during the convoy:

"One lone patriot on an overpass, holding a flag in the wind, speaks louder than a hundred who stand in a crowd."

I held onto that.

At just after eight o'clock, I shouldered my pack, adjusted my livestream mount, and nodded to Mr. T. "Let's do this."

He eased *Beechy* forward, the engine rumbling low behind me as I took my first step of the *Grey Wolf Walk Across America for Freedom*. The chat crackled to life in my earpiece—moderators reading comments, voices of encouragement, and the familiar banter of people who'd been following me since The People's Convoy.

"You're cutting corners already, Grey Wolf!" someone teased as I crossed a gas-station lot to rejoin Highway 50.

I smiled. The trolls were quick, but my moderators were quicker.

***

The Flag and the Faith

A few miles out of Carson, I saw it—a weathered American flag lying half-tangled in sagebrush along the roadside. I stopped, lifted it free, brushed away the dust, and tucked it carefully into my pack.

It felt like a sign.

I wasn't just walking across the desert. I was carrying that rescued flag—and, in a way, carrying the heart of the nation that had begun to forget itself. Every blister, every drop of sweat, would mean something if I could help remind people who we are meant to be.

The Nevada sun rose higher. I switched out my walking shoes—one of three pairs sent by supporters who wanted to help me make it across the miles. *Each pair felt like a prayer beneath my feet.* Still, by mid-afternoon, a blister began to swell under my right foot. The pain was sharp, but I didn't pop it. It was proof of purpose.

By late day, Mr. T radioed that the Calvary Chapel Dayton Valley had agreed to let us park overnight. We pulled in as the light faded, grateful for power, shade, and a place to rest. I stretched my sore legs and whispered a quiet prayer of thanks. The first day was behind me—and with it, the loneliness that had marked its start.

Sunday Morning

The next morning, the sound of car doors and greetings drifted across the lot. Church members were arriving for Sunday service. Mr. T and I stepped out with our coffee mugs in hand, Abby on a leash, unsure of what to expect.

A man waved us over. "You must be the walking veteran we heard about!"

Soon we were inside sharing breakfast—bacon, egg, and cheese ciabattas, hot coffee, and conversation that felt like home. Pastor Garry Leist asked if we could stay for worship, but I explained that I needed to start early, before the sun turned the asphalt into an oven.

He showed Mr. T where the water hose was, and while Mr. T began filling *Beechy's* fresh water tank, I went back inside to thank the people I'd met that morning.

Before we left, Pastor Garry gathered several members in a small circle beside *Beechy*. Together we prayed for strength, safety, and endurance—for the road ahead and for the mission itself. They even prayed for Abby, which made me smile.

As I walked away from the chapel, the morning wind carried Pastor Garry's final words after me: "Keep walking for truth."

***

Stagecoach and the Symbols

By mid-morning, the road shimmered with heat. Highway 50 stretched endlessly east—wide, quiet, and humbling. Mr. T kept a steady distance behind me in *Beechy*, the *"Caution: Walkers for Freedom Ahead"* sign bungee-corded to the back.

That was when I saw it—just one small shoe lying on the white stripe of the shoulder of the highway. A small child's sneaker—sun-bleached, dust-covered, and heartbreakingly out of place. I stopped and stared at it for a long moment. The sight felt out of place, but it carried weight, as if it had something to say.

It felt like a message whispered by the road itself: *Save the children.*

I said a small prayer before continuing.

By the time I reached the town of Stagecoach, the pain from my blister was burning. I decided to stop for the night. We parked beside the Rose Creek Pizzeria—the new name for what had once been the Wagon Wheel Pizza and Grill. The young woman inside smiled when I walked in.

"You've been expected," she said. "Would you like your wings and pizza?"

My daughter had called ahead and ordered dinner for us. When I walked in, *the smell of melted cheese and garlic hit me like grace itself*. Mr. T and I sat down to eat, while Abby stayed in *Beechy*—quiet, tired, and content, curled up on her blanket between the front window and the curtain where she could keep watch, *finally at peace after a long, hot day*.

I talked with the staff about the Walk—about freedom, faith, and the courage it takes to stand firm when the world goes quiet. They listened with open hearts, nodding as I spoke. One man said softly, "Keep it going, brother. We need this."

I kept the livestream running through dinner, reading comments from supporters as they came in. A few familiar names from the convoy appeared in the chat. "Congrats on the day, brother—have a great 4th tomorrow," one wrote. Their words felt like a handshake across the miles.

That night, as the desert cooled, Mr. T and I sat outside under a canopy of stars. The generator hummed, Abby curled beside my feet, and the road ahead felt less lonely than before.

***

The Fourth of July

Day Three began with the sunrise and the sound of my own voice singing The Star-Spangled Banner. It was July 4th, and I couldn't think of a better way to celebrate than by walking for freedom.

The chat on Discord was alive—supporters howling, laughing, sharing stories from across the country. Someone played "Wake Up in the USA," a song by my friend Steve Spurgeon, who'd told me I could use it as my Walk's theme. His message reached me that morning:

"Thank you for your sacrifice to remind Americans what it takes to keep our nation great. Your willingness to give yourself for others is the foundation of this country. God bless you on this great day in our nation's history."

A white pickup passed, flags streaming behind it. For a moment, the sight took my breath. I raised my walking stick in salute. *That image—the flags, the sunlight, the hum of the road—captured everything I was fighting for.*

Along the shoulder, two blue crosses rose from the dry ground, surrounded by faded flowers. I stopped, laid my hand on one, and bowed my head for Stacy and Katrina.

***

The Mustangs

A few miles before Silver Springs, movement flickered along the fence line to my left—wild mustangs. Six, maybe seven, easing out of the sage. They stayed with me for nearly a mile, heads high, breath pluming, hooves whispering in the sand. They didn't spook; they matched my pace like an honor guard, close enough for me to hear the soft snort of the lead mare. It felt like the desert itself had stepped out to walk beside me—quiet affirmation that the road, and the reason, were right. When they finally veered off toward the hills, just before the Silver Strike Casino—our stop for the night—I lifted my walking stick in thanks and kept moving.

Later that afternoon, my brother Jim surprised me. He pulled up with supplies—socks, drinks, bandages—and a grin that seemed to say, *You're really doing it.*

We visited for a while inside *Beechy*. The hum of the A/C and the murmur of the livestream filled the space. I looked down at my bandaged foot and laughed softly. "Only 3,000 more miles to go."

Jim said,

"Then keep walking."

That night, as I lay in my bunk, the pain in my foot pulsing with each heartbeat, I thought of the lone flag I'd rescued, the prayers from strangers, and the mustangs I'd seen pacing the fence line that afternoon —wild, free, untamed.

Each one seemed to whisper the same thing:

Keep going. Don't stop. The road is long, but you are not alone.

Chapter 22 – The Weight and the Worth

The next morning, I woke before sunrise and lit the burner under the old Mr. Coffee, coffee pot that didn't need electricity. The slow hiss and gurgle as it brewed filled *Beechy's* cabin with that familiar, comforting smell. Mr. T was still stretched out on the dinette bed, snoring softly. Abby, my little French Bulldog and constant companion, hopped down from my bunk and padded to the door. I grabbed her leash and took her outside for a morning walk.

The air was cool and still, the desert washed in pale lavender light. Abby sniffed at the sagebrush and looked up at me as if to say, *We've got miles ahead of us, Dad. Funny how we imagine what our pets are thinking — and sometimes, we're probably right.* The eastern horizon glowed pink behind the mountains, a quiet promise that the sun was coming. For a moment, I just stood there listening — to nothing but the faint breeze and the slow rhythm of my own heartbeat. That kind of stillness only exists before the world fully wakes.

When I came back inside, Mr. T had two mugs waiting on the table.

"You're up early," he said.

"Couldn't sleep," I answered. "Too much road waiting out there."

I started walking around nine. I didn't know exactly where we'd stop that night — only that my right foot was in bad shape. The blister from the day before had spread across the ball of my foot and between my toes. But pain is a poor excuse to stop when your cause is freedom.

My supporters were already on Discord, checking maps and calling ahead to find safe pull-offs. I started the livestream, adjusted the camera, and took my first steps — one, *then the next* — *the rhythm of persistence.*

To distract myself from the pain, I sang: *King of the Road, God Bless America*, even a few old hymns. Sometimes I recited the Constitution, one article at a time, explaining how it still mattered. Out here, *every mile was an essay, every word a reminder that the power of the people isn't granted by government — it's protected from it.*

The desert wind carried my voice back in faint echoes. The steady crunch of gravel underfoot became its own kind of music. Each step hurt, but each one also meant I was still alive, still standing, still moving forward.

***

The Fifty Horse Ranch

By late afternoon, the sun beat down hard enough to turn the asphalt silver. My crew had found a stop east of Silver Springs — the Fifty Horse Ranch in Lahontan Valley. From the road, the horizon looked empty, so when they said, "You're almost there," I laughed into my mic.

"Almost? You've been saying that for two miles!"

I figured they were teasing me. But then, over the next rise, I saw it — a scattering of outbuildings, fences, and a shimmer of movement beyond the sage. Horses. Real, living symbols of freedom.

As I drew closer, they lifted their heads and began trotting toward the fence line. They followed me step for step — curious, proud, untamed. I raised my walking stick — the one topped with the carved grey-wolf head gifted to me by Truckin-Girl before the walk began — and nodded in silent thanks.

The sight felt like a blessing, as if the land itself were saying, *Keep going, Grey Wolf. You're not alone.*

At the ranch house, a woman and a man came out to meet me.

"I was told we could park here for the night," I said.

She smiled. "Park by the side gate. You're welcome here."

Mr. T eased *Beechy* into place and fired up the generator, then took Abby to explore the shade near the corral while I sat inside, shoes off, foot throbbing. My Discord moderators checked in about the day, and we laughed about the endless climb. *"Over the Hill,"* someone joked — the perfect title for the day's blog. They weren't wrong. The stretch between Silver Springs and Fallon was nothing but hill after hill, each one testing willpower more than muscle. One climb ran nearly four miles without a break in the incline. At one point, I even walked backward up a section just to work different muscles and give my blistered foot a chance to breathe.

As the sun went down, the horses grazed quietly against the red horizon. I felt that deep pull of gratitude — for shade, for water, for purpose. *It wasn't comfort that mattered anymore; it was meaning.*

***

Over the Hill and Into Purpose

The next morning, I brewed another pot of coffee and stepped outside with Abby. The first light poured over the desert like liquid gold. I said a short prayer for strength, then started walking again. From there to Fallon, the road leveled out — long, flat stretches that sometimes narrowed until there was barely a shoulder at all. Mr. T followed at a crawl behind me, the sign bungee-corded to the back of *Beechy*: *CAUTION: WALKERS FOR FREEDOM AHEAD.*

For a while, I walked along the old Carson Highway, which paralleled Highway 50. Beechy rumbled steadily behind me, loyal as ever. Around midmorning, we pulled off at a Nevada Department of Transportation yard to rest and eat, parking just outside the gate. The quiet hum of trucks in the distance mixed with the dry desert breeze — a reminder that even on lonely roads, life keeps moving.

Each mile felt like a sermon in motion. I talked to my livestream audience about loyalty — not to parties, but to principles.

"You don't vote for someone because they've got an R or a D by their name," I said. *"You vote for the person who stands by the Constitution and represents you — not their own power, or the power of a party."*

Someone on Discord read me a message from a viewer:

"Grey Wolf, you should run for office. You're already leading."

I laughed. *"I'm not walking for office. I'm walking for accountability — for reminding folks that government isn't our master, it's our servant. That's what this flag means."*

Still, the thought lingered. I had considered running for the State Assembly in District 27 — not as a Republican or Democrat, but as an Independent. Not to join the system, but to challenge it from within.

That day, Sasnak — a fellow convoy driver and streamer with a huge following — called me live while I was walking. His voice came through the earpiece:

"Ron Coleman, you're on the air, brother."

We talked about my reasoning for the Walk — how one man's steps can still echo louder than a thousand opinions. The chat lit up, messages flying across the stream. Supporters howled, others prayed, and a few skeptics asked hard questions. I welcomed them all. That's what freedom sounds like — disagreement without destruction.

Later, as I walked, I shared something that had been weighing on me.

"Many people think mandates are laws," I said. "They're not. Laws come from legislators — the ones we elect and hold accountable through the process of debate and vote. Mandates bypass that process entirely. And when we forget that distinction, we surrender power that was never the government's to begin with."

I paused for a moment, then added what had become one of my most repeated lines:

"Mandates are nothing more than directives from someone in a cigar smoke–filled room."

It wasn't anger that drove the words — it was conviction. Out here, with nothing but the desert wind and the sound of cars and trucks rushing by, I had all the clarity a man could want. *Freedom wasn't abstract. It was sweat, pain, and personal responsibility under a hot Nevada sky.*

***

Fallon and the Healing

By late afternoon, my moderators told me the next stop was secured — the Golden Gate Truck Stop in Fallon. I radioed Mr. T and limped the last few miles. When I got there, a kind woman came out to greet us.

"You're the one walking across America?"

"Yes, ma'am."

She smiled and introduced herself as the manager. "You can stay as long as you need."

We parked near the rear edge of the lot and leveled *Beechy*. I peeled off my shoes and socks and winced. The blister had split wide — raw and red — and my right knee ached from compensating. I didn't know it yet, but I had torn the meniscus — an injury that would eventually require surgery. For now, all I could do was rest and trust that the road would wait.

That evening, one of my moderators surprised us with a DoorDash delivery — enough Mexican food to feed an army. Burritos, enchiladas, chips, and salsa. Mr. T laughed as I unpacked it.

"Holy smokes! Look at this spread!" he said.

"Yeah," I laughed. "Guess this'll cover a few days."

I stayed in Fallon for a couple of days, doing everything I could to heal. Each morning, I sat outside with Mr. T and Abby, coffee steaming in the cool air, watching the sunrise spill across the open desert. Sometimes I felt guilty for resting, but my supporters reminded me — *even soldiers pause to regroup*. Their messages — prayers, jokes, and encouragement — became medicine.

Truckers honked as they rolled past. Some stopped to shake my hand. Others dropped off supplies — water, socks, and once, a bag of fresh fruit. A few came just to talk about what freedom meant to them. Their stories reminded me that the Walk wasn't about one man. It was about all of us who still believe *liberty is sacred* — and that America, for all her flaws, is worth every mile.

When I finally stood again, testing my weight, the pain was sharp but manageable. I looked east toward the long stretch of the Lincoln Highway shimmering in the afternoon light. The road called — quiet, patient, insistent.

I knew I couldn't walk every mile of America.

But I could walk the ones that mattered.

And that was enough.

Chapter 23 – Lessons from the Road

***

The Road Calls Again

I woke one morning in Fallon with a heaviness I couldn't quite name. It wasn't exhaustion — I'd known that kind of fatigue before — it was guilt. Not guilt toward my supporters or the mission, but toward something deeper, almost spiritual. It felt as though the road itself was calling me back, whispering that my work wasn't finished.

Mr. T must have felt it too. Before dawn he was already moving quietly through *Beechy*, tightening straps, checking fluids, and setting mugs on the table. The coffee pot hissed on the burner, its rich smell wrapping the cabin in warmth. We hardly spoke — words weren't needed. The desert was waiting, and we both knew it.

By the time the first hint of light touched the sky, Abby was at the door, eyes bright. She looked back at me as if to say, *Well, Dad? Time to go to work.*

We rolled east out of Fallon while the stars still held their ground against the coming sun. I started walking in the half-light, each step slow and deliberate, testing the mended skin of my foot. The first quarter mile was agony — the kind that makes your teeth clench and your breath go shallow. Every pulse of pain rose through my blistered sole and up into my knee. But pain was part of the tuition the road charged for its lessons, and I wasn't about to skip class.

Five minutes in, something fluttered in the wind ahead — an American flag flying at half-staff on a tall pole. I stopped, placed my hand over my heart, and recited the Pledge of Allegiance aloud into the quiet and my livestream. My voice came back thin against the emptiness, but it felt right — a promise renewed before the day began.

Later that morning, Mr. T pulled *Beechy* off to the side of the road and parked near an abandoned looking building so I could rest. I must've dozed off for a bit, because the next thing I remember is hearing voices outside the RV. When I looked out, the Sheriff of Churchill County was standing there, talking with Mr. T.

Ron "Grey Wolf" Coleman with Beechy, Fallon, NV. — July 2022

"You folks okay?" the Sheriff asked.

Mr. T told him about the Walk and handed him one of our cards. The Sheriff smiled and said, "Appreciate what you're doing. I'll check out the site when I get to the station."

***

Salt Wells

As the sun climbed, the desert began to shimmer — bands of gold and silver stretched across the horizon. Mr. T and I were talking on the radio about a clearing ahead. "Salt Wells," he said. It wasn't a town anymore — just a scatter of pale earth and half-buried foundations.

"This is far enough for today," he said gently.

He was right. My heart wanted to keep walking, but my body was done arguing. I leaned on my walking stick and stared at a rusted spigot jutting from the ground, its orange handle frozen — a monument to something that used to flow freely.

"Let's get you inside," Mr. T said. He helped me up the steps of *Beechy*. My sock peeled away from the raw skin beneath, and the pain pulsed like fire.

On Discord, my moderators' voices filled the cabin.

"Ron, you've got to stop and heal."

"Try castor oil — old-school trick, but it works."

Castor oil? I almost laughed. It sounded like something your grandmother kept next to the cough syrup and the good scissors. But at that moment, I was willing to try just about anything.

We decided to backtrack.

***

Return to Fallon

Beechy rumbled to life, groaning like she shared my reluctance. We rolled west through the wavering heat until the first gas-station sign rose from the desert like a promise. Fallon again.

We stopped at a drugstore — bandages, Tylenol, and one small bottle of castor oil. Mr. T went in and did the shopping. At the counter, he told the clerk about the walk and handed her one of our cards.

Back at the Golden Gate Truck Stop, relief and frustration tangled in my chest. I hadn't wanted to return, but sometimes the road sends you backward so you can move forward stronger.

Inside a small café next door, the waitress noticed the lettering on *Beechy's* back.

I told her about the *Grey Wolf Walk Across America for Freedom* — about faith, country, and the belief that ordinary Americans still have the power to stand tall.

She poured me a cup of coffee and said, "You're welcome here anytime."

That small kindness lifted the weight I'd been carrying. The road might wound you, but it also sends healers when you need them most.

Later that morning, I joined my moderators online to plan the next steps. One supporter — the same one who had come up with our slogan just before the walk began — reminded me of it again. It seemed even more fitting now, almost like a prayer in motion:

"Walk for a mile, or walk for a while."

It became our rally cry. The Walk didn't need a crowd marching coast to coast; it needed hearts awakened — even if only for a single mile.

***

Visitors and Volunteers

A few days passed in recovery. The castor-oil treatment was working better than any pharmacy cream. Then, one night around 10:30, a pickup rolled into the lot pulling a small enclosed trailer. Out stepped a woman from Pennsylvania — a retired nurse and one of my longtime online supporters.

"I couldn't just watch from home," she said. "I had to come help."

Her trailer was packed with donations: cases of water, medical supplies, even a cooler full of meat. She cleaned and dressed my foot like she'd been doing it her whole life.

"You're not losing time," she said while wrapping the bandage. "You're gaining strength."

The next day, the three of us — Mr. T, the nurse, and me — sat outside under a broad blue sky. Abby lay between us, her chin resting on her paws. *Beechy's* generator hummed softly in the background. For the first time in days, peace replaced pain.

That night, after the nurse turned in, I stayed outside and watched the stars stretch across the desert. Each one felt like a prayer pinned to the heavens — tiny lights of encouragement sent by people I might never meet but who somehow believed in what I was doing.

***

The Preamble in the Desert

A few mornings later, we returned to Salt Wells — the very spot where I'd stopped and turned back to Fallon. This time, I was ready — or at least I believed I was. We left before dawn, the stars hanging low in a sky brushed with steel and indigo. The air bit at my cheeks — sharp, clean, and alive — like the breath of a new beginning.

At 4 a.m., my headlamp carved a narrow cone of light across the sand as I stepped back onto Highway 50. *Beechy* followed at a slow crawl, her headlights glowing like a faithful guardian behind me.

When dawn finally broke, something strange shimmered off to my left — shapes rising from the sand like bones. At first I thought they were old fence posts, but as I got closer, the shapes became letters — massive words formed from black rocks.

It was the Preamble to the U.S. Constitution, built into the desert itself by artist Michael Dax Iacovone.

I slowed to a stop and began reading aloud:

"We the People of the United States, in Order to form a more perfect Union, establish Justice, insure domestic Tranquility, provide for the common defense, promote the general Welfare, and secure the Blessings of Liberty to ourselves and our Posterity, do ordain and establish this Constitution for the United States of America."

The words echoed over the sand and through the livestream. For a long moment, the chat went silent. Even through a phone screen, people felt it — that stirring reminder that We the People are the foundation, not the footnotes.

I turned the camera toward the stones. "This," I said quietly, "is what I'm walking for."

As I shouldered my pack again, the pain in my foot returned, but it carried a different weight. It wasn't suffering — it was sacrifice. Every step felt like another signature on that old parchment promise.

***

Encounters on the Highway

Around mid-morning, two cyclists appeared on the horizon, pedaling west from the direction of the rising sun. As they drew closer, I could see the flags stitched to their packs — travelers from the Netherlands, riding from Denver to San Francisco. They slowed as they came alongside me, their accents light and cheerful against the quiet stretch of desert.

"Where are you headed?" one asked.

"Washington, D.C.," I said.

Their eyes widened. "On foot?"

I nodded. "For freedom."

They exchanged a quick glance, then both smiled. For a few minutes we talked — about the road, the heat, and the strange kind of peace that comes from long miles under an open sky. Before leaving, they shook my hand and wished me luck. Then they leaned back into the wind, their wheels humming softly as they disappeared into the shimmer ahead.

I stood there for a while, watching until they were only specks in the light. There was something poetic about it — two men from another country crossing paths with one man walking to remind his own what freedom really costs.

Moments like that were small, but they mattered. Each encounter, each shared word or wave, was proof that the message was moving farther than my own two feet ever could — carried by the people who felt it, one conversation at a time.

Two golden eagles circled above us for a stretch, wings glinting in the sun. I took it as a sign — freedom keeping watch.

***

Sand Mountain

By late morning the pale rise of Sand Mountain shimmered on the horizon — a dune so massive it looked like the ocean had turned to glass mid-wave. The closer I came, the more it felt like a living thing — breathing heat, waiting.

My knee throbbed with every step, and the blisters on my foot pulsed like live wires beneath the skin. Still, the words of the Preamble echoed in my head: *"…secure the Blessings of Liberty to ourselves and our Posterity."*

Mr. T was waiting in the parking lot near the entrance to Sand Mountain. He leaned out the door as I limped up beside *Beechy*.

"You want to keep going?" he asked.

I looked past him to the great white dune glowing under the noon sun, then to the highway stretching east — steep, relentless, and shimmering with heat.

"Not today," I said. "We'll start the climb before sunrise — beat the heat."

Mr. T parked Beechy in a cracked, sun-faded lot and shut her down for the evening. The air outside buzzed with the steady chorus of crickets, punctuated by the rush of passing cars and trucks on the highway. Abby stretched out beside my chair, her head resting on her paws, eyes half-closed but always alert — the kind of calm that only comes when a long day is finally behind you.

The desert cooled from gold to purple to deep indigo. Mr. T sat beside me with his ever-present mug of coffee. "You know," he said, "every time you stop, you find something sacred out here."

He wasn't wrong. Out here, the classroom had no walls. The lessons came in wind and silence, in pain and persistence, in strangers who stopped to say thank you and in friends who drove across the country just to lend a hand.

The climb waiting for me wasn't just another stretch of highway — it was a test of everything I'd claimed to believe. Faith, endurance, and the courage to keep moving when logic said stop.

Somewhere out there, beyond that shimmering dune, lay the next mile of the *Grey Wolf Walk Across America for Freedom.*

And at four a.m., when the stars still ruled the sky, I would rise to meet it.

Chapter 24 – The Climb and the Healing

The morning began in still darkness at the cracked asphalt parking lot outside Sand Mountain Recreation Area. Highway 50 hummed nearby — a thin ribbon of sound threading through the emptiness. Truck lights slid like ghosts across *Beechy's* faded paint. Inside, the air carried the quiet scent of coffee, canvas, and desert dust. It wasn't luxury, but it was home — and this small patch of Nevada pavement was where faith would once again meet endurance.

I woke around 3:45 a.m., my alarm set for four — the kind of waking that isn't startled or sleepy, but summoned. Abby stirred on her blanket beside me, watching as I tied my shoes, eyes bright in the dim light. Frenchies don't wag tails; they speak with their whole faces — a low whuff of breath, a tilt of the head that said, *you really mean it, don't you?*

Mr. T slept in the bunk right up until his alarm buzzed — the rattle of the coffeepot beside it finished the job.
"Already moving?" he muttered.
"Gotta beat the heat," I said, handing him a mug.

Outside, the stars hung heavy and bright — cold pinholes over an ocean of sand. We moved through our ritual in silence: tightening straps, filling the CamelBak, checking the livestream gear, and offering a short, wordless prayer while leaning against *Beechy's* side. The metal felt cool and steady beneath my palm.
"May the Lord keep our minds clear and our steps steady," I whispered.

The first few steps away from the RV were small and careful, testing the knee that still ached from the Salt Wells stretch. The original blister on my right foot had hardened, but new ones had begun to rise around it. Pain had become a companion — not welcome, but honest. The desert accepted no lies.

The road bent upward almost immediately, curling around the base of Sand Mountain's entrance. The dune glowed pale under the moonlight — a frozen wave waiting to break. The air lingered in the seventies, the coolest it would be all day. A dry breeze slipped down the slope, carrying the taste of salt and dust. *Beechy* followed behind at a crawl, headlights painting the shoulder gold.

Around 4:40 a.m., the livestream caught signal. Familiar names flickered across the chat, faithful as the morning star. Then one viewer typed: "Grey Wolf, what's your cause?"

I smiled into the darkness — a question, maybe a challenge, maybe a troll. "Glad you asked," I said, the words steadying my pace. "My cause is to get people off the couch and engaged again. We all know something's wrong with this country. We're supposed to be a land for the People, and it's on us to keep it that way — to keep America constitutionally sound. Government doesn't grant rights; God does. That's why they're unalienable. Its only duty is to protect them."

A pause. Then hearts and flags scrolled up the screen. Someone wrote, 'Walk loud, Brother.' The digital fellowship felt like a campfire carried in my hand.

I kept talking, more to them than to myself. "I saw it during the convoy — miles of overpasses filled with flags, people crying because they finally felt seen. It wasn't politics; it was grief. We've mourned freedoms lost, and we're ready to stand. This walk is proof that one step still matters."

The chat quieted, reverent. The desert listened too.

Half an hour later, Weather Cat — one of our moderators — posted a fact:
'Fairview Peak quake, 1954. Magnitude 7.3. The ground lifted six feet in seconds.'

I stopped to read it aloud. The idea of the earth shrugging under pressure like that hit me deep. "Guess even the land can only take so much before it moves," I said. "Sometimes shaking is the only way to find a new balance."
Mr. T chuckled through the radio. "Preach it, boss."

The grade steepened. Sweat traced cold lines down my spine. I tasted metal in the air — the ghosts of old mines scattered through the hills. A century ago, prospectors chased silver up these same ridges, gambling with heat and thirst. Their mule trails had long turned to dust, but the will that drove them felt close. Maybe the American spirit is hereditary — passed down through calloused hands and stubborn hearts.

As dawn began to edge the horizon, the world shifted color. Shadows bled into violet, then pink, then the fierce white of daybreak. The air warmed quickly; the smell of creosote rose like burnt honey. I adjusted the straps on my pack and found rhythm: step–walking stick–breathe.

Somewhere behind me, a truck honked twice — a salute. I raised my walking stick — *Wolfie* — the rescued flag from the first day still tie-wrapped to its shaft, without turning. Encouragement from strangers felt like wind at my back.

By mile three the road curved toward the top. My lungs worked like bellows. The livestream buzzed again — a question scrolling up: *"Can you explain Article 5?"*

"Happy to," I said, pausing to sip water. "Article 5 of our Constitution explains how we amend it. Most people think only Congress can propose changes, but there's a distinctive or in the text — and that *"or"* matters. Beyond it, the Constitution makes clear that the states can propose amendments too. The Founders gave us that option — a Convention of States — so power could never bottleneck in D.C. It's our safety valve when government forgets who it serves."

Another viewer teased, *'Grey Wolf University open for business!'* "Every mile's a classroom," I laughed, breathing hard. The rhythm of teaching helped drown out the burn in my legs.

Around mile four, the wind came alive — a hot blast funneled through the canyon, pushing grit into my teeth. The grade eased near the crest. My steps shortened but quickened; each footfall thudded with purpose. Heat waves shimmered ahead like water that wasn't there.

Mr. T's voice crackled through static: "You're close, boss. Half a mile to the top."

That half mile lasted forever. Then the road leveled, the horizon exploded open, and light poured over everything — an ocean of golden basin stretching as far as the mind could imagine. I stood still, chest heaving, both hands on *Wolfie*. The silence roared.

Mr. T pulled *Beechy* to the shoulder and climbed out with Abby. We said nothing at first. The view said it all — the cost, the grace, the endlessness. Abby stood between us, tongue out, sides heaving. I knelt and poured a capful of water into my palm for her; she lapped it, nose twitching. "Good girl," I murmured.

I pulled off my shoe and checked the blister. Torn again, but not bleeding. I cleaned it, re-taped, and cinched the laces tight. Pain, discipline, motion — the trilogy of the walk.

We started down the eastern side, legs trembling from the descent. The Fairview Range rippled ahead — scarred hills telling stories of time. I thought of the quake again, the land itself reshaped. Maybe that's what this walk was doing to me: breaking, shifting, settling into something new.

By the time we reached the valley floor, the sun was merciless. Heat shimmered off the asphalt; mirages wavered like ghosts of water. I focused on my breath — count four in, four out — the soldier's trick for endurance. On my screen, the chat buzzed with encouragement. I couldn't read through the sweat, but I heard their words relayed by my moderators in Discord.

Then, at 8:29 a.m., my GPS ticked over — 100.0 miles — just as we approached the Nevada state monument on the valley floor. I stopped mid-step, laughed out loud, then took two extra paces just to be sure. "That's one hundred miles, folks!" I said into the mic. "Since Carson City. Every tenth counted — and yes, I'm counting."

Applause emojis and digital fireworks filled the feed. I planted *Wolfie* upright against *Beechy*, the flag from Day 1 fluttering in the heat. "First milestone," I said. "And the Republic's still worth every step."

The heat burned through my sleeves; the flag's shadow quivered at my feet. Mr. T filmed from the monument pull-out, grinning wide. Abby pawed at the sand, then flopped down in it, indifferent to history. I closed my eyes, whispered thanks. Pain, pride, prayer — all folded into a single heartbeat.

We lingered a while. I thought about that first morning leaving Carson City — the empty streets, the weight of beginning. One hundred miles later, that weight had become momentum. This wasn't a stunt; it was a covenant renewed with every sunrise. My right foot burned from fresh blisters, a reminder that progress always costs something. I ended the day's walk there and climbed into *Beechy*, bound for Middlegate Station and a much-needed rest and healing.

When I sat in the seat, the heat seared through my pants. I laughed and yelped at once. "Holy heat!" Mr. T turned up the fan, steering us east. The old RV groaned but rolled steady. Outside, a blue highway sign read: *Next Services – Middlegate Station, 10 Miles.* Beneath it, someone had scrawled in marker: *The Loneliest Road in America.*

"Let's see what lonely looks like," I said.

The desert unspooled in shimmering ribbons. Every few miles, a rusted relic appeared — a broken signpost, the skeleton of a windmill, the ghost of a homestead long forgotten. We passed the turnoff to the Fairview Peak trailhead — the birthplace of Weather Cat's earthquake lesson. The ground out there had once leapt six feet in a heartbeat; now it lay still as prayer. I pointed to a set of crumbling stone walls in the distance. "Old Pony Express stop," I said. "1860s."

Mr. T nodded, watching the heat warp the ruins into mirage. Those riders once carried freedom in saddlebags; I carried it in a livestream and a heartbeat. Same message, new medium.

A thought began to brew — something about that connection between old riders and new messengers. I'd let it steep a while before putting it into words.

We reached Middlegate close to noon — a crossroads more myth than town. A single gas pump stood beside the old station, its paint sun-blistered, numbers faded. The restaurant's porch sagged under the weight of history and a thousand signed dollar bills pinned to the ceiling inside. The air smelled of fry oil and sagebrush.

Then came the whir of a ceiling fan and laughter from inside the saloon. A sign on the door read: Population 17 (Formerly 18).

We were welcomed like family — a woman sliding me a glass of iced water before I could order. Abby stayed in *Beechy* with the A/C humming.

Mr. T raised his glass. "To the first hundred," he said.
I clinked mine to his. "And to the miles still waiting."

Outside, the sun hammered the desert white. But in that worn old outpost — between the hum of the fan and the kindness of strangers — healing had already begun.

Chapter 25 – Bubba's Return and New Roads

After several days resting at Middlegate Station, the desert began to whisper again — that familiar tug of unfinished miles. My foot was nearly healed, my knee steadier, and the calluses had hardened just enough to promise endurance. It didn't feel right to sit still, but I knew better than to push forward too soon. Every step taken before my body was ready would only cost me more down the road. So I waited.

Each day at Middlegate gave my body time to knit itself back together. Nine blisters had bloomed on my right foot since Sand Mountain — the old ones hardened to callus, the new ones raw and angry. I had twelve pairs of walking socks — breathable, quick-dry — and rotated them religiously: one pair drying in *Beechy* while the other carried me a few miles before switching again. Even in rest, there was discipline.

Middlegate Station felt like a desert outpost turned sanctuary. The place had a small bar, a restaurant that smelled of fry oil and nostalgia, a few motel rooms, and a gas pump that looked older than I was. Travelers stopped for fuel, bikers for beer, truckers for stories. Patriots came and went — each one curious about the signs on *Beechy*. Some just nodded in quiet respect; others asked questions, leaning in close like they were joining a secret.

One evening, as the sun bled into the Stillwater Range, I joined a group of folks on the porch. The wind hummed through the power lines while conversation drifted between politics, faith, and family. That's where I met Ryan — a young Marine veteran with eyes that had seen deserts of a different kind.

We swapped service stories, Air Force to Marine Corps, two branches meeting halfway across the sands. When I told him about the blisters that refused to heal, he nodded, then jogged to his car and came back holding a small unopened tin.

"MelaGel," he said, tapping the lid. "We used this stuff in Iraq. Tea-tree oil base. Works on blisters, burns, whatever the desert throws at you."

I twisted it open. The smell was sharp, medicinal, and somehow hopeful. I rubbed some on, thanked him, and we talked about purpose — how battles change shape but never really end. Before he left, he pulled out a fifty-dollar bill and pressed it into my palm.

"I want to give to what you're doing," he said. "Keep walking."

That small act — the balm, the money, the belief — felt like a relay hand-off between soldiers of different wars. Within a day, the soreness eased. Healing came not just from medicine, but from mercy.

That night Ryan and his friend Janet joined Mr. T and me for dinner. The conversation turned to America, to censorship, to truth. Janet shook her head. "People just don't see what's happening."

Ryan added quietly, "Maybe they don't hurt bad enough yet."

Their words stayed with me long after the plates were cleared.

Later that night I joined a livestream panel hosted by Texas Girl on her ONEVoice channel — a reunion with friends from the convoy: Sasnak, Mud Pig, Lit'l Blinky, DiegoTV, and Lisa the Mayor. We laughed like family around a digital campfire, teasing, remembering, plotting new ways to keep the flame alive. It felt good to belong again.

By morning, the air had cooled, and the pain in my foot was almost gone. The MelaGel had worked wonders. I sat on the step of *Beechy*, coffee steaming in the dawn light, Abby sprawled beside me watching the occasional car drift by on Highway 50.

That's when I knew — it was time to move again.

***

The Return to the Hundred-Mile Marker

"Let's head back," I told Mr. T. "Ten miles west — that marker where we hit a hundred."

He folded the map with a grin. "Test run?"

"Exactly. Ten miles of truth."

We packed up early, the wind already rising off the valley. Clouds stacked high over the Stillwater Range, bruised with coming rain. Gusts shoved *Beechy* sideways as we rolled west, her frame groaning like an old ship at sea.

"Feels like she's sailing, not rolling," Mr. T muttered, gripping the wheel.

"Just keep her straight," I said, watching tumbleweed sprint across the asphalt.

When the wind and rain finally calmed, we pulled into the turnout near the Nevada State Historical Marker — the spot we'd claimed as the hundred-mile point. The air smelled of wet sand and ozone.

I'd told my daughter I'd be there that morning. Her reply had been short: There's a surprise on the way.

I figured it was a package from a supporter — maybe supplies. I wasn't ready for what came instead.

Out of the wavering horizon, a familiar car turned off the highway, gravel crunching under its tires. I blinked once, twice. It was Bubba's sister.

She stepped out, wind tugging at her hair, eyes red from miles of thought. In the back seat were her two kids, and next to them sat Bubba's old dog, tail-thumping against the seat.

My throat tightened before she even reached me.

We hugged and stood together for a long time, the silence saying what words couldn't. Finally, she spoke. "I'd like to see where my brother passed."

I nodded and led her into *Beechy*. The air inside was still, heavy with memory. She sat on the edge of the step by the drivers seat, by the doghouse — the same spot where Bubba had taken his last breath — and rested her hand on the driver's seat.

When we approached her car, she pressed a small velvet pouch into my palm. "He wanted to be with you on this journey," she said softly.

Inside was a two-inch urn — Mossy Oak Camo veins like lightning frozen in metal. Simple. Dignified.

I carried it inside, along with a framed photo she'd given me. Bubba grinning wide under the words In Loving Memory. I mounted the photo above the doorway, right where he had drawn that last breath, and fixed the urn to the dash with double-sided tape.

"Ride with us, brother," I whispered.

Outside, her kids were playing with Abby, laughter chasing away the weight of the moment. She waved once before driving off, dust curling up behind her car like a benediction.

Inside *Beechy*, the urn gleamed in the afternoon light.

***

The Walk Back to Middlegate

By midday, the sun was brutal again. I should have rested, but stillness didn't feel right after that kind of goodbye. I laced up my shoes, and stepped out. Mr. T idled behind me in *Beechy*, hazard lights blinking against the glare.

The road stretched straight as faith — ten miles of shimmering heat and silence. My shirt clung to my back, each step a quiet negotiation between pain and pride.

At mile five, I stopped for water, lungs working like bellows under the desert sun. The climb had turned brutal, the air hot enough to sting when I breathed. By mile seven, the world shimmered and tilted — the kind of dizzy where your body starts whispering warnings you can't ignore. I climbed into *Beechy*, collapsed into the seat, and let the fan blast across my face before stretching out on the bunk. My heart hammered; the edges of my vision pulsed white. For a few long minutes, I just lay there, waiting for the world to steady. I took a couple of acetaminophen and closed my eyes, letting the medicine dull the headache that had come on hard. For about an hour, I rested — letting the air conditioner hum, the heat fade, and my body remember itself. Heat stroke had brushed close enough to remind me who was really in charge out here.

When the dizziness eased, I drank more water, said a quiet prayer, and stepped back onto the asphalt. Three miles remained — over the summit and down toward Middlegate Station— and I meant to finish them, slow and steady. By late afternoon the mirage of Middlegate

Station shimmered ahead — a cluster of roofs swaying in the heat haze. Mr. T honked once and passed me, parking near the old porch.

"Hundred and ten miles," he said with a grin. "And Bubba's along for the ride."

Just outside the café, an older couple stopped me near the old gas pump. "You're the one walking across America?" the man asked.

"Yes, sir," I said. "For freedom — and for the people."

His wife frowned gently. "We think things are fine. Why walk at all?"

I smiled. "That's what makes this country great — we all get to think for ourselves."

No need for debate. Respect was its own victory.

That night, as the desert cooled, I sat at the dinette inside *Beechy* with Abby on my lap and a sweating can of diet soda in my hand. Bubba's photo glowed faintly above the door — that easy grin, unbroken by time. For the first time since Hagerstown, I felt them all with me again — every voice, every mile, every friend. The road had taken much, but it gave back too.

***

Cold Springs Station

Two mornings later, I woke with no pain. The blisters had sealed into callus. Ryan's balm had done its job. I told Mr. T we'd start small — ten miles at a time until the road felt kind again.

After breakfast with the folks at Middlegate Station, we packed up and rolled east. The highway was empty but for dust devils and distant mirages.

That day's goal: Cold Springs Station — a speck on the map about thirteen miles away, a remnant of the old Lincoln Highway and the Pony Express.

The first few miles were quiet. Then, at a small turnout, I stopped beneath a tall cottonwood plastered with hundreds of shoes dangling from its branches — *the famous Shoe Tree*.

I told the story to the livestream: a newlywed couple arguing on their wedding night; the husband flinging his wife's shoes into the tree; their reconciliation; the annual ritual of tossing new shoes as a symbol of love unbroken.

"Guess we all leave something hanging in the branches," I said.

Viewers dropped heart emojis and laughing faces in the chat.

Later, the horizon shimmered with movement — a solitary figure pedaling toward me. For a second I thought it was a cyclist. Then I realized he was balancing on a single wheel.

A unicycle.

He coasted to a stop beside me, grinning under his helmet. "Name's Christian," he said, breathless but cheerful. "Been riding from Michigan to Reno."

We laughed at the absurd beauty of it — two travelers propelled by willpower alone. After a quick photo and handshake, he rolled off westward, the desert swallowing his silhouette.

Man from Eaton Rapids, Crosses Paths w/ Grey Wolf. — July 2022

As the miles passed, I shared another story with the stream — one from childhood. "A father and his three sons," I began. "He told them

142

that whoever could break the bundle of sticks he'd tied together would inherit all his possessions when he passed. The first son tried, but no matter what he did, he couldn't snap them. The second son gave it a go — same result. Then the third son stepped forward, untied the bundle, and broke each stick one by one. When he was done, he looked at his father and said, 'I've broken them all.'"

I let the story hang for a moment before finishing: "A single stick is fragile, but bound together, they can't be broken. That's America. That's what we've forgotten."

Someone in chat typed, Amen to that.

By early afternoon, I reached mile marker seventy-six. My body had said enough. Mr. T noted the spot in his log as I climbed into *Beechy*, every muscle humming with fatigue. He eased the old girl back onto the highway and drove the last few miles to Cold Springs Station.

The engine's steady hum filled the silence between us as the desert slipped by. Each mile felt like exhale after strain — a quiet surrender to the road ahead.

Chapter 26 – Cold Springs Station (The Brotherhood Forms)

Cold Springs Station sat at the base of a wind-carved ridge — a scatter of weather-worn cabins, an RV park, and a small restaurant that smelled of burgers, coffee, and old wood. The place looked like a mirage someone had hammered into permanence.

The owner, a broad-shouldered man named George, stood behind the bar when I walked in.

"You're Grey Wolf, right? Been following you online," he said with a grin. "Got an RV spot out back for you. Dinner's on the house — two nights if you need 'em."

His wife, Barbara, looked up from behind the counter and smiled.

"We even serve tater tots," George added with a wink — a callback to the livestream a few days earlier.

We all laughed. Their kindness felt like a handshake from the universe itself.

By noon, the desert heat shimmered off *Beechy's* roof like a living flame. George had set us up behind the restaurant — water, power, and a view that stretched all the way to the Stillwater Range.

I spent the early afternoon inside, perched at the bar with a sweating glass of diet soda beside my plate, chatting with my livestream family as they checked in from across the country — even a few from Canada and Australia. Their voices filled the quiet between the clink of glasses and the creak of boots on the old wood floor, turning that dusty Nevada outpost into something that felt a little like home.

Outside, life moved slow — the kind of slow only the Nevada desert knows.

A woman returning from the laundry room stopped short when she spotted *Beechy*. Mr. T was at the back, stowing a few things in the rear compartment and adjusting the walk sign, while Abby napped inside out of the heat.

"Okay," she said, smiling, "I've got to ask — what is that rig, and what's that sign about?"

Mr. T grinned like a proud mechanic showing off a classic.

"She's a '67 Beechwood," he said. "And the man inside — Grey Wolf — he's walking across America for freedom."

Her eyebrows lifted. "No kidding? I've got to tell my husband about this."

With that, she turned and disappeared toward the trailer parked beside us.

The sun slid lower over the ridge, softening the light and easing the heat that had baked the gravel all day. The scent of sage drifted in on a light breeze, and the hum of cicadas filled the stillness. Later that evening, as the air turned gold and long shadows stretched across the lot, Mr. T and I set up our folding chairs in front of *Beechy*. Abby lay between us, belly pressed to the cool earth, her legs stretched out front and back — those back ones we always called her "drumsticks," because when she stretched them out like that, they looked exactly like turkey legs fresh from the oven.

A tall man with kind eyes and the easy stance of someone who's lived a lot of road walked over carrying a folding chair under his arm.

"You must be Grey Wolf," he said, offering a hand. His grip was firm, steady. "Name's Tom — my wife, Patty, said I had to come meet you guys."

We shook hands, and he unfolded his chair beside ours like we'd done this a hundred times before. The conversation came easy — stories from service days, the long miles that teach you patience, and the kind of talk that happens only between people who understand silence.

He listened more than he spoke, but when he did, it was with the weight of someone who thought before he talked. We drifted from war stories to faith, to how quickly this country seemed to be forgetting what both were built on.

Somewhere in the middle of that, he glanced toward the road and said quietly, "You heading back out tomorrow?"

146

"Yeah," I said. "Goin back to mile marker seventy-six — need to finish that stretch back to here before breakfast."

He nodded once, like he'd already made up his mind.

"I'd like to walk with you," he said.

I looked at him for a moment, surprised, then smiled. "You'd be the first," I told him. "And I'd be honored."

He leaned back in his chair, the faintest grin tugging at his face. "Then it's settled. What time do we head out?"

"I want to be at the mile marker by four a.m.," I said.

His expression shifted to mock horror. "Four? I usually don't see daylight until ten." He paused, then laughed and added, "But all right — let's do this."

Above us, the sky turned from gold to violet, and the first stars began to show — the kind of quiet agreement that needs no more words.

We began at 3:49 a.m., headlamps cutting thin tunnels of light through the mist. The desert was alive around us — chipmunks darting at the edge of our beams, coyotes yipping from the dark, wings brushing the night air above. It felt good to share that with someone who understood — the rhythm of footsteps, the echo of purpose, the sound of creation moving with us.

We talked about service, faith, and what it means to love a country enough to fight for it twice — once in uniform and once on foot.

At dawn we paused near the ruins of the old Pony Express Station. Stones stacked by hands long gone still held their shape against time and wind. I read aloud from the weathered marker:

"Cold Springs Station was built in 1861. Riders changed horses here; travelers found meager lodging. The telegraph soon followed, and by 1869 both were gone, replaced by the railroad."

We stood quietly for a moment.

"Hard to imagine carrying freedom in saddlebags," Tom said.

"Now it rides on the airwaves," I answered, tapping the livestream mic clipped to my pack.

We took a photo together — two veterans, two generations, one purpose.

By 7:12 a.m. we reached Cold Springs Station again. George and Barbara were waiting outside, clapping as we came into view.

"Breakfast on us!" Barbara called.

Inside, over bacon, eggs, and coffee, we talked about the miles ahead — fifty empty miles before the next town.

"It'll get lonelier from here," George said, half warning, half benediction.

That afternoon I sat outside *Beechy*, watching as the wind moved across the valley where the Pony Express once rode, where telegraph wires once sang, and where now only the wind carries messages. Bubba's urn caught the last light, glinting with quiet strength — Mossy Oak brown turned to gold.

We planned to stay two more nights. The next morning I'd rise before dawn to walk another ten or so miles east before returning to camp.

By midday, Tom — now "Whiskey Tango" — strolled over to where Mr. T and I sat in our folding chairs. The heat shimmered above the gravel; Abby panted softly at our feet.

Whiskey folded his arms, the brim of his cap shadowing his eyes. "I'm going to talk to Patty," he said. "See if she wants to join the *Grey Wolf Walk Across America for Freedom.*"

I nodded, hopeful. "She strikes me as the type who'll say yes."

He smiled, gave a short wave, and headed back toward their trailer.

Evening settled slow and honey-colored over the desert, the long Nevada light stretching the shadows clear to the horizon. Around six or seven, just before the sun slipped behind the ridge, Whiskey walked back across the gravel. Mr. T and I were in our usual spots, Abby standing between us.

He carried his chair, unfolded it, and sat down with that same steady calm.

"Well," he said, a grin tugging across his face, "we're going to join you in this mission."

We stood, shaking hands. "Welcome aboard," I told him.

He nodded. "We'll leave for Fallon first thing in the morning — grab supplies — and be ready to roll east after that."

The light caught *Beechy's* side, turning her weathered paint to gold. The wind that swept down from the ridge was warm and clean, carrying the scent of dust, sage, and promise.

For the first time in days, the road ahead felt open again — wide, waiting, alive with possibility.

The *Grey Wolf Walk Across America for Freedom* would no longer be a solitary march.

It had become a convoy of hearts and histories — bound by purpose, by freedom, and by the hum of the American highway.

I was no longer walking alone.

Chapter 27 – The Gathering (A Convoy of Patriots)

Morning came cool and bright over Cold Springs Station, the air carrying the scent of sage and the promise of distance. For the first time in a long while, I knew I wouldn't be walking alone much longer. Whiskey Tango and Miss Patty were heading to Fallon that morning to stock up on supplies and get ready to join the walk in full.

Mr. T moved *Beechy* toward the highway as I laced up my shoes. The plan was simple: I'd walk about ten miles east, mark the spot, and return to camp by afternoon.

Beechy rumbled behind me, Mr. T keeping a slow, steady crawl as my rolling shadow. The desert spread endless and pure—the kind of quiet that asks for reflection and gives it back with clarity. Even with my Discord channel live in my ear and moderators calling updates from across the country, there was no substitute for the sound of shoes on pavement and the voice of faith that lives somewhere between your steps.

The miles passed steady beneath my feet. When I stopped to rest, the heat shimmered off the asphalt. A message cracked through my earpiece—one of my moderators.

"Grey Wolf, we've got news."

I grinned. "Go ahead."

"Texas Girl and her family are packing up. They're leaving Oregon—heading your way to join the walk."

The words hit like a gust of wind at my back. The movement was growing again. It wasn't just a man, a dog, and an RV anymore—it was becoming a convoy of believers.

By mid-morning, I'd logged around ten miles. Mr. T marked the spot in his log, and I climbed into *Beechy* for the ride back to Cold Springs Station. The hum of the engine and the smell of hot dust filled the cabin—simple sounds of forward motion.

When we pulled back into the station, Whiskey Tango and Miss Patty had already returned from Fallon, their pickup poised to hitch to the trailer and ready for the road. They waved as we rolled in.

That evening, the desert cooled and the light went soft. I sat outside watching the stars gather one by one. Whiskey Tango walked over and leaned on *Beechy's* corner beside me.

"Patty's in," he said, smiling. "We're in this for the long haul."

I nodded, feeling that familiar lump rise in my throat. "Welcome to the family."

***

The Third Morning

Cold Springs Station woke early, the scent of coffee and bacon drifting through the thin desert air. George had breakfast waiting for us —our final meal before rolling east. We ate at the counter, trading hugs and laughter with the kind of people you feel like you've known your whole life.

"Be safe out there," Barbara said as we stood to leave. "And don't forget—tater tots on the house when you make it back this way."

By seven, *Beechy* was idling out front, the sun already warming the gravel. Whiskey Tango and Miss Patty pulled their rig into line behind us, ready to begin their first day on the road with the *Grey Wolf Walk Across America for Freedom.*

We drove back to the mile marker I'd stopped at the day before. Whiskey Tango joined me on foot, and Miss Patty took the wheel of their pickup, following close behind *Beechy.* The desert morning spread wide and pale around us. Conversation came easy—two veterans swapping stories, trading lessons from the service and the road, talking about faith, duty, and the Constitution. Every word seemed to find its echo in the vast Nevada sky.

By late afternoon, the heat pressed down like a weight. We'd covered about ten miles when we stopped at the old Overland Stage Station site near New Pass, its crumbling stone walls half-swallowed by time. The air was dry and still, the kind that carries history in silence. It felt right —like the road itself was offering us a place to rest. We parked the rigs, set up camp, and watched the sun dip low behind the ridge. That night, the stars looked close enough to touch.

State Historical Marker, New Pass Station, NV. — August 2022

***

Across New Pass

The next morning, Whiskey Tango's feet told the story of too many hard miles too soon. Deep blisters had bloomed between his toes—raw, red, and angry. He gave a sheepish grin, waved off our concern, and said, "Guess I'll drive chase for a bit."

I handed him the tin of MelaGel the Marine, Ryan, had given me back at Middlegate Station a few days earlier. Whiskey turned it over in his hand, smirking. "Marine Grease!" he declared, and we both laughed.

So that morning, Miss Patty laced up her shoes and walked beside me while Whiskey handled the support vehicle behind *Beechy*. The climb out of New Pass was long and steady, the wind rising and falling in slow breaths across the desert basin.

As we were climbing the last half mile to the summit, *Beechy* suddenly died. Mr. T came over the radio as I walked ahead.

"She's dead, boss — I can't get her to start back up!"

Miss Patty and I turned and walked back toward her, Whiskey Tango pulling up close behind. Worry was written on everyone's faces. I climbed inside and pulled the doghouse cover to take a look.

While I worked, a traveler towing a boat pulled over and called out to Mr. T and Whiskey. He said he'd drop the boat up ahead and come back with a chain to tow us if needed.

As soon as he pulled away, I popped off the distributor cap and saw the problem — the points weren't opening. I loosened the set screw with a screwdriver, adjusted the gap with them high on the lobe, tightened it back down, and replaced the cap. Then I turned the key.

Beechy roared back to life like nothing had happened. Barely five minutes had passed since she'd died.

We started walking again just as the man returned in his truck, chain ready. When he saw *Beechy* running, his eyes went wide. Mr. T and Whiskey were just as surprised. We all laughed, waved our thanks, and he headed east, still smiling.

As I watched him drive off, I thought — that's what this is all about. Total strangers, willing to give their time to help someone on the road.

We made good time that day, covering about eight and a half miles before cresting Mount Airy Summit. The descent on the eastern side opened into a long, level turnout—flat, wide, and perfect for camp. Mr. T parked *Beechy*, and Whiskey Tango eased their trailer in behind him. The silence that settled over the basin was the kind only the high desert knows—vast, clean, and infinite.

***

The Arrival

As the last of the light faded, a distant pair of headlights shimmered on the horizon. They grew brighter, cutting through the dusk until they turned into our pullout. The sound of gravel under tires carried across the still air.

It was Texas Girl, Juniper, and their two kids—Collier and McKenzie—arriving at last after their long drive from Oregon. Along the way, they'd stopped at my home in Sun Valley to pick up a few supplies, then again at Cold Springs Station to collect the donations George and Barbara had been keeping safe for us.

When they stepped out, Abby barked and the camp came alive. Laughter, hugs, and pure relief filled the air under the rising moon. Texas Girl wrapped me in a tight hug, tears bright in her eyes.

"We made it," she said.

Juniper grinned and patted the grill in the back of his trailer. "We're eating right from now on," he said with a wink.

We all laughed, the promise of that simple line warming the cool desert air. No food was cooking yet—just the smell of road dust, sage, and the hum of excitement that comes with new arrivals. The kids chased Abby around the vehicles while the adults unfolded chairs and settled near the lantern glow. Out there beneath a sky heavy with stars, the *Grey Wolf Walk Across America for Freedom* felt alive again—a family forming in the middle of nowhere.

***

The Morning of the Hat

The next morning broke clear and full of promise. The chill from the night still hung in the air as coffee brewed and conversation drifted between the three rigs. Sunlight spilled over the ridge, washing the turnout in gold.

As everyone packed up camp and prepared for the day's walk, Texas Girl called out behind me, "Hey Grey Wolf, let me see that hat."

I turned, puzzled, and handed over my Air Force veteran cap. With a grin, she pulled a wide-brimmed straw hat from behind her back, the underside lined with the stars and stripes.

"This," she said, "is what you wear from now on. And I promise— the desert sun won't catch it on fire."

It was a playful nod to the livestream chatter from earlier days, when one viewer warned that a straw hat wouldn't survive Nevada—that it might just spontaneously combust in the desert heat.

I laughed and set the new one on my head. It felt right—light against the sun, bold against the horizon. From that morning forward, the hat —and Wolfie, my walking stick—became symbols of the journey.

On Discord, Mama Wolf asked if she could lead a prayer before we started the day's walk. We gathered in a circle, each of us resting an arm over the next person's shoulder, heads bowed as her voice came through the speaker on my phone—steady, heartfelt, and strong.

I handed Texas Girl my Canon camera. "You're our photographer now," I said. She smiled, adjusted the strap around her neck, and began snapping photos before we even hit the road.

Miss Patty joined me for the first stretch that day, with the kids, Collier and McKenzie, taking turns beside us. *Beechy* rumbled behind, Mr. T keeping her steady at a crawl, while Whiskey Tango followed in their pickup, still tending to his blistered foot. Up ahead, Juniper led the way in his Nissan Armada, the Stars and Stripes snapping in the wind from his window.

The morning air was cool and easy. We walked east along Highway 50—eleven and a half miles ahead to Jacobsville Park and Ride. After a few miles, Miss Patty swapped places with Whiskey Tango so he could walk while she drove chase. The kids rode ahead with Juniper. The rhythm of footsteps and conversation carried us through the valley, the desert waking slowly around us.

Somewhere near the halfway mark, a call came through my earpiece: Texas Girl and Juniper were going to drive ahead and set up camp at Jacobsville Park and Ride. "We'll have dinner ready when you get there," she said.

By late afternoon, we crested the final rise and caught the first scent of cooked pork drifting on the wind. Flags waved ahead in the fading light, and the sound of laughter floated across the highway. Juniper had the grill up—pork roast, baked potatoes, and corn sizzling over the hot coals.

We ate beneath a sky painted violet and gold. The kids ran between the rigs, Abby trotting after them. It felt less like a mission that night and more like a family gathered at the edge of the world.

***

The Road to Austin

The following morning dawned bright and windless. Our goal was simple—a seven-mile walk into Austin, Nevada. Texas Girl and Juniper went ahead to check in at the RV park and get camp ready.

Mr. T frowned as *Beechy* idled beside the shoulder. "She's not running right, boss," he said. He was right—the old girl was starting to stumble, misfiring. I thought those points had failed again.

Still, we pressed on. The road stretched straight toward Austin, the sun climbing higher with every mile. By the time the town came into view, *Beechy* was coughing hard, her engine stumbling like an old soldier pushing through the last march. Out of the shimmer ahead, Texas Girl and Juniper appeared—coming out of the east to meet us. They turned around and pulled in front, dust curling in their wake.

Texas Girl leaned out the window and called, "We've got our spot secured! We're heading back to finish setting up."

I nodded and told Mr. T to follow them in—no sense risking a breakdown before town—while Miss Patty kept steady behind me and Whiskey Tango in the chase truck.

When I finally reached the campground in Austin, the rest of the crew was waiting. Juniper already had the grill going, and the smell of barbecue drifted through the mountain air.

That evening, we ate like family—pork, and baked beans —laughter and stories blending with the hum of cooling engines.

The *Grey Wolf Walk Across America for Freedom* had become something larger than any one of us: a convoy of families, veterans, and believers moving east together, bound by faith and purpose.

As the stars came out and the firelight flickered across those faces, I thought:

This is what freedom looks like—ordinary Americans standing together, no matter where the road leads.

Chapter 28 – The Trial in Austin

The morning after we reached Austin, *Beechy* refused to wake up right. She'd start, cough, and die again—rocking in her parking spot like she was gasping for air. Mr. T looked at me through the windshield, his face saying what neither of us wanted to: something serious was wrong.

I climbed inside, pulled the doghouse cover, and took a look. The distributor points were still where I'd set them after the breakdown west of town, but they looked rough—pitted and burnt. Maybe that was it. Maybe she just needed another tweak. For two days, I chased small fixes that went nowhere. Each time she'd turn over, sputter, and die. The old girl was tired.

On the third day, I got word that Ron and Geri were on their way from Oregon. They were longtime supporters—patriots who had followed the *Grey Wolf Walk Across America for Freedom* from the beginning, sending signs and supplies along the way. When they arrived, they pulled in grinning, arms open like old friends.

"Let's get this girl running again," Ron said, patting *Beechy's* side.

He volunteered to drive all the way back to Fallon—and then again to Battle Mountain—to fetch tune-up parts: spark plugs, wires, a distributor cap, and a fresh set of points. That's the kind of people we had on our side—folks who saw a need and filled it without being asked. Geri, a retired nurse with a heart as big as Nevada, brought along three pairs of new walking shoes for me. "Figured you could use some fresh tread," she said with a wink.

When Ron and Geri came back with the parts, I swapped everything out—new plugs, new cap, clean points. Still no difference. *Beechy* coughed, shook, and died again. By then, I knew it wasn't electrical. This was deeper.

So I rolled up my sleeves, pulled the valve covers, and took a look inside. That was when I saw it: several rockers were loose, and beneath them, four bent and broken pushrods. That was bad—real bad. The only way that happens is when valves stick. After sitting all those years before the walk, her old oil must've turned to molasses in the guides. I felt my stomach sink. This was going to be a fight.

Everyone's faces told the story—concern, frustration, maybe even doubt.

"She done, boss?" Mr. T asked quietly.

"No," I said. *"Not yet."*

We didn't have the luxury of calling a mechanic. If *Beechy* was going to live again, I had to do it myself.

Whiskey Tango drove to Eureka for some specialized tools—a valve spring compressor, valve stem umbrellas, and anything else we could scrounge.

While he was gone, I kept the mission alive through livestreams, talking with folks across the country about the Constitution, government overreach, and mandates that had never made sense. The trolls came in waves—mocking, jeering, trying to drown out the message—but my moderators were faster. Sharp as ever, they booted the troublemakers before they could do real damage. I wasn't about to let negativity derail what we were building.

When Whiskey returned, tools in hand, I got to work. I pulled the intake manifold to remove the bent and broken pushrods that couldn't be lifted through the head openings. Each lifter came out next— cleaned, checked, and reinstalled. The cam lobes looked solid, smooth, and unscored. Then, one piston at a time, I rotated the engine to top dead center and used the new spring compressor to pull the valve springs.

That's when the real work began. I gently clamped a pair of vise grips to the top of each valve stem, heated it carefully with a propane torch, and hit it with bursts of brake cleaner. The old oil and sludge bubbled up from the guides around the stems like tar melting under fire. Slowly, stubbornly, the valves began to free—one by one—until they moved smooth and clean, as if waking from a long sleep. Intake and exhaust, every single one got the same treatment. When they finally moved true, I slipped new umbrella seals over the stems, seated them snug, and reinstalled the cleaned springs.

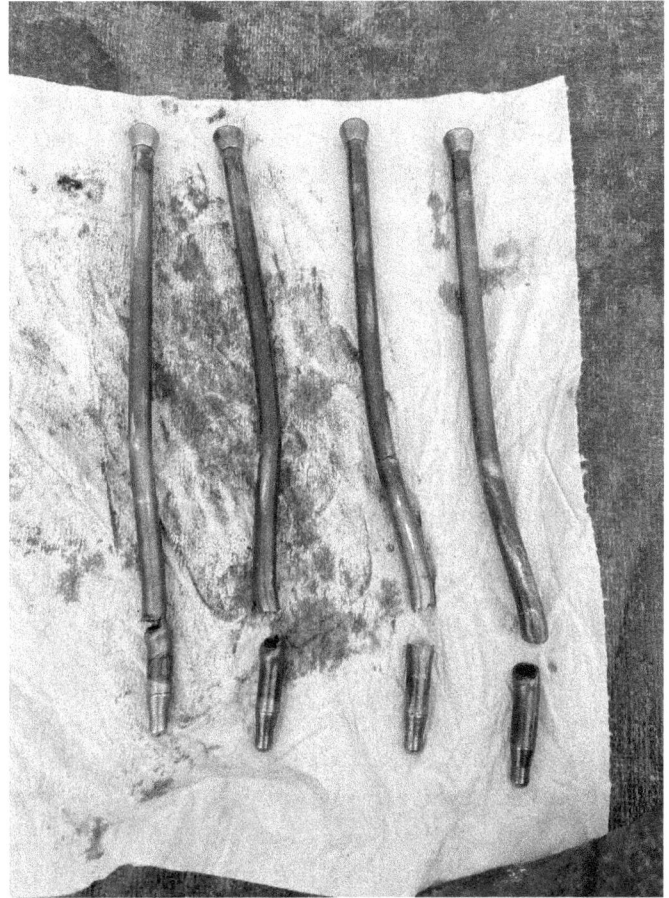

Bent and broken push rods, Austin, NV. — August 2022

When it was done, I stood back and looked at the valve train. For the first time since the breakdown, it looked alive again—bright metal where there had been darkness, motion where there had been none.

The others watched from the shade, shaking their heads in disbelief.

"Can't believe you're doing that right here in camp," Whiskey said. "Got no shop, no lift, and you're rebuilding an engine."

I laughed. *"Just wrenching, brother. She'll run again."*

Finding parts was another challenge. The valve seals were easy enough—universal umbrellas that Whiskey tracked down at an auto parts store in Eureka—but the pushrods and gaskets for that old 318 Poly were another story. I finally located a set through a performance company that specialized in racing engines. They could sell the pushrods individually, but the intake gaskets came with a catch: I had to buy the entire gasket kit—intake, exhaust, valve covers, head gaskets, everything. I placed the order and waited.

Two days turned to five. Then eight. Shipping delays stacked up like bad news. The company sent a replacement shipment using another carrier, and then a third. Days rolled by. The second week came and went, and still nothing.

While we waited, life went on. Whiskey and Miss Patty spent most nights out at the petroglyphs, camping under the open sky. They'd come back into Austin now and then for supplies and to do laundry—or for barbecues that stretched late into the evening. One night, Juniper cooked enough chicken to feed a small army, the smoke drifting across the lot while we laughed under the canopies. Abby snoozed by my chair, her little Frenchie ears twitching at every sound.

Some days, thunderstorms rolled through hard and fast—the kind that come roaring down off the mountains like they've got a grudge. One storm hit so strong that Texas Girl and Juniper's canopy, tied down to *Beechy's* front bumper with weights on each leg, lifted clean off the ground and slammed into her nose. The crash made us all jump. It nearly shattered the front window. When it was over, the canopy was a wreck, but *Beechy* stood firm, battered but unbroken. We pulled the twisted frame away in the rain, laughing at the absurdity of it all.

Those storms mirrored the mood—frustration, waiting, hope. Every day I'd check the tracking numbers, praying for good news.

The storms also showed us where *Beechy's* window seals had seen better days—Mr. T's bed was soaked. The next morning, we pulled the large side window out and went to work. I scraped out the old, cracked sealant and cleaned the frame down to bare metal. We replaced the rusted screws with stainless ones I'd stashed in the back compartment and laid fresh butyl tape to seal it tight against the elements.

Everyone pitched in. Juniper handled the fine cleaning, same steady precision he'd shown on the intake manifold. Texas Girl pressed the tape and started the screws. Mr. T wiped down the glass and siding until they gleamed. When we finished, the window looked—and sealed—like new.

Finally, on day sixteen, a brown delivery truck pulled into camp. The driver handed me a box, grinning. "You the guy with the old RV?"

I was.

I tore it open like a kid on Christmas morning. Inside were the pushrods and gaskets I'd been waiting for.

We worked fast—Whiskey handing me tools, Mr. T fetching oil, everyone doing something. I installed the new push rods, replaced the seals, put the intake back on, and changed the oil and filter. *Beechy* looked whole again, ready for one last test.

After all that, one more of the three shipments finally showed up, and Texas Girl and Juniper found another—sitting a block away on the step of an abandoned trailer, soaked from the rain. When I called the company to let them know, they told me to keep everything. The carriers had already paid for their mistakes. I told Mr. T, "We got spares!"

Late that night, with everyone gathered around, I climbed into the driver's seat and turned the key. For a heartbeat, there was silence. Then the engine caught—smooth, steady, strong. The sound echoed through the little valley like thunder after a storm. We all cheered. Even Abby barked.

The next morning, we test-ran her over to the laundromat on the west side of town. She purred the whole way there and back—not a hiccup. The old girl was back.

While the parts delay stretched on, we kept the mission alive. I held a small rally at the park next to the swimming pool—Austin's little town square. Not many people came, but it didn't matter. The ones who did brought stories, prayers, and faith. The RV park we'd been staying in doubled as the local church, and some of the congregation had become part of our extended family. They told us they prayed for us every night, and I believed them.

As the days in Austin were being counted, we were restless. The climb east out of town was one of the toughest stretches on Highway 50—sharp switchbacks, no shoulders, blind turns. Just weeks earlier, a driver resting in the pull-out near the summit had been killed by a truck that lost control. Deputies and troopers warned us about the danger.

We decided to tackle it smart. One morning, Miss Patty, Whiskey Tango, and I set out to hike the grade while Juniper ran chase, leapfrogging back and forth with a flashing light and warning signs on his vehicle. Texas Girl and Mr. T stayed at camp, monitoring traffic on the radio. Every time a car or truck came through town, they'd call up its color and direction. Juniper either dropped back to slow traffic or moved ahead to warn oncoming drivers. It worked perfectly.

The air thinned with each switchback. My blisters had long since turned to calluses, and I felt stronger than ever. I was nearly power-walking up the mountain until Whiskey called out, "Hey, Grey Wolf, mind slowing down a little?" So I did. We stopped for water from time to time, laughed, and caught our breath.

When we finally reached the summit, the weather station came into view—a tall tower with spinning sensors against the blue sky. We stopped for a photo and sent it to one of my moderators, WeatherCat, who'd been giving us real-time weather reports from that very station. "Reporting live from your tower," I said on the livestream. She loved it.

The next day, one of my online supporters, Maryann, drove into Austin to meet us in person. She brought cookies and prayers, worried we might have to end the walk. "We'll get *Beechy* running again," I told her. "We're not done yet."

I made an announcement video on my social media—a message I'd been shaping since Cold Springs Station, and since my visit to the U.S. Senate back in March, when I'd first told them I was acting as a modern-day Pony Express rider for the people. I'd promised the folks in Cuba, Missouri that I'd carry their messages all the way to Washington, D.C.—and now I was ready to make that pledge part of the walk itself.

A supporter soon sent an authentic-looking replica of a Pony Express mailbag to Austin. From then on, I would begin collecting letters, notes, and cards from people we met along the way—each one a voice, a hope, a reminder that America still had something to say. When the bag would fill, I'd transfer the contents into burlap sacks and keep the pouch ready for more—bound eastward to D.C., messages from the heartland carried one step at a time in the spirit of those who once rode for freedom.

By day seventeen, we had her buttoned up and ready. I checked every connection, ensured every bolt was tight, and wiped my hands clean of weeks of grease and dust. That evening, under a sky streaked with gold and violet, we gathered for one last meal before the road called again. Juniper fired up his grill-top pizza oven, improvising with flour tortillas in place of dough. They came out crisp and golden, bubbling with cheese and laughter in equal measure.

Smoke drifted through the still air, laughter rising between the distant echoes of sonic booms from military jets breaking the sound barrier overhead. For all the setbacks and frustration, those eighteen days had forged something deeper than we'd had before—a family, a faith, and a reason to keep moving.

When dawn came on the eighteenth day, *Beechy* sat idling like new, her engine smooth and proud. We broke camp quietly, each of us knowing what it had taken to get here. Mr. T climbed into the driver's seat, Abby curled on the dinette, and I stood for a long moment looking east— toward the mountains that waited, toward the next stretch of road.

Austin had been a trial by fire—a lesson in patience, in perseverance, and in what it means to rebuild. The road ahead wouldn't be easier, but as *Beechy* rolled out, smooth and steady, I smiled.

Freedom doesn't quit—it rebuilds.

Chapter 29 — The Road Reawakens

The days in Austin rolled on like the desert wind—slow at first, then steady with purpose. Even while waiting on *Beechy's* parts, I couldn't stay still. Some mornings, I laced up my shoes and walked the stretches I'd left unfinished before the breakdown.

There was the day Miss Patty and Whiskey Tango joined me for the climb to the weather station atop Austin Summit, with Juniper running block in the car ahead. Another morning, I started from that same station and pushed ten more miles east, while Juniper and Texas Girl marked my finish point for the day before driving us all back to Austin.

We'd fallen into a rhythm: Juniper and Texas Girl would drive me out at dawn, I'd walk until the afternoon heat began to rise, and they'd bring me back just as the sun dipped low. Along the way, they'd pull over with a cold pouch of Pickle Juice—my secret weapon against the cramps that came with the miles and the heat.

One walk brought Ron and Geri from Oregon out to join me. Ron walked a mile or so beside me and Whiskey Tango, shoes crunching the shoulder gravel, while Geri followed behind in their pickup. Whiskey Tango and Miss Patty took turns walking and driving chase, while Juniper ran point up front, alerting oncoming traffic to our presence, communicating with handheld radios. It felt like a convoy again—each of us playing our part, each of us keeping the mission alive.

Another day, Whiskey Tango and I spotted a hand-painted sign along the highway: Fresh Eggs – Self Serve. We stopped and found a cooler full of farm-fresh cartons, with a small box beside it for payment. Out here, honesty was still the rule, not the exception. We left our cash, loaded up a few dozen, and brought them back to Austin—proud as if we'd struck gold. Juniper, our camp cook, was ecstatic at the find.

Then came the walk that would mark a milestone in more ways than one—Day 29 of the *Grey Wolf Walk Across America for Freedom*, July 30, 2022. (It also happened to be my moderator Giovanna's birthday.) I started at Mile Marker 37 in Lander County, heading east toward the Hickison Petroglyphs. It was an eleven-and-a-half-mile stretch, and somewhere around mile 5.8, I crossed my bicentennial distance marker

—two hundred miles on foot since the beginning, every one of them earned the hard way.

There was no cell service that day, so I filmed short clips on my phone instead of livestreaming. The road was quiet except for the wind and the rhythm of my steps. I walked alone, but never lonely. I thought of everyone who'd stood on overpasses waving flags, of the veterans who'd shared their stories, and of the promise I'd made—to carry their voices east.

As I climbed the grade toward Hickison Summit and the weather station at the top, Juniper followed behind, calling over the radio, "Fourteen-minute miles on a seven-percent grade—you're a beast!" he said. I just laughed.

When I reached the summit, Juniper drove ahead to the Hickison Petroglyphs to drop Texas Girl at the entrance—camera in hand, ready to capture the moment. After a few photos beneath the open Nevada sky, we visited with Whiskey Tango for a few moments before heading back to Austin. The day ended in stories, laughter, and that rare kind of stillness that only comes after a long, hard climb.

That would be my last walk during the repair stretch. From then on, I turned my focus fully to Beechy—repairing, livestreaming, and planning the next phase. Somewhere in those days, I made the Pony Express announcement, explaining how I'd begin collecting letters and messages from Americans along the way to be delivered by hand to Washington, D.C. The mission was growing, and so was its meaning.

***

Beechy Is Peachy — August 10, 2022

We had finished the repairs to Beechy and tested her as well—she was strong again. The next morning, we packed camp and rolled east.

We stopped again at that little egg stand, exchanged our empty cartons for full ones, left our money, and were just climbing back into our rigs when a van pulled across the road and parked. Out stepped a woman named Cindy, all the way from Maine.

She smiled and said, "You invited me."

It took me a second to realize she meant my livestream. She'd heard my call to join the walk, packed her van, and driven clear across the country. She'd already logged plenty of miles on her own—starting in Maine—but now she wanted to be part of the Grey Wolf Walk.

We convoyed together to the Hickison Petroglyphs, where Whiskey Tango and Miss Patty were already camped. Later that afternoon, Whiskey Tango, Cindy, Road Runner (Mackenzie), Shot Gun (Collier), and I explored the petroglyphs together. I took photos and explained to the kids what the site represented—stories carved in stone, left behind by those who came long before us.

We spent the night there, the desert quiet settling around us. The next morning, we began our route from the Hickison Petroglyphs to Mile Marker 2 in Eureka County—just over ten miles. Six of us took turns walking: Cindy, Miss Patty, Whiskey Tango, Road Runner, Shot Gun, and me. The road shimmered in the August heat, thunderheads stacking high on the horizon.

Weather Cat kept us posted on the storms through Discord. During one break, I asked the group whether we should stop early. The words had barely left my mouth when lightning struck the exact stretch of road we'd have been walking on if we hadn't paused.

We looked at one another and laughed. "Guess we got our answer," I said.

***

Good Vibrations — August 11

We drove from Mile Marker 2 to the Bean Flat Rest Area that evening, racing the thunderstorm rolling in from the west. Lightning flashed across the desert sky as we set up camp, the wind carrying that sharp, scent of ozone and rain.

By morning, the storm had passed, and we returned to Mile Marker 2 to pick up where we'd left off. Sometime during the night, someone had quietly dropped off a crate full of canned goods beside the trailer. No note, no name—just kindness left behind in the dust. We never found out who it was, but it reminded me how generosity still runs deep in this country.

That evening, a van pulled in carrying Frank and Mikayla, visitors from Germany traveling across the American West. We invited them over to our camp for dinner—pork with cowboy beans and cornbread, cooked up by Juniper. They'd never tasted cowboy beans or cornbread before, and the look on their faces after the first bite made us all laugh. That unmistakably American flavor—smoky, sweet, and hearty—won them over fast. Everyone went back for seconds.

We talked for hours under the stars. Frank said that freedom was the most important thing in his life, that in Germany, fear and politics had taken too much of it during the pandemic. He told me that revolutions don't have to be violent—they can be peaceful, led by the people themselves.

I smiled. "Sounds like we're walking the same road, my friend."

As I sat by the fire that night, I thought about how far we'd come—from broken parts in Austin to new friends at Bean Flat. The road was alive again.

Faith, freedom, and fellowship had carried us this far, and the horizon was wide open once more.

That night at Bean Flat, the desert stars burned brighter than ever. The air was cool, the silence deep, and I could feel the miles behind us settling into something larger than the walk itself. We had rebuilt more than an engine—we had rebuilt faith, trust, and purpose.

Tomorrow, the road would rise again, stretching east toward Eureka and beyond. Beechy was strong, the crew was ready, and the mission was alive.

The *Grey Wolf Walk Across America for Freedom* was no longer just a journey.

It was a movement—one step, one story, and one heart at a time.

Chapter 30 — The Turning Point

The morning sun rose soft over the Bean Flat Rest Area, the sky still streaked from the night's storm. *Beechy* was pointed east again, the road stretching ahead in quiet invitation. We made good time that morning, covering about ten and a half miles before thunder began to rumble across the distant ridges. The desert light shifted fast—gold to gray— and then the rain came hard. We had no choice but to take cover.

We climbed back into *Beechy* and pushed ahead about six miles to a wide dirt pullout called the Roberts Creek parking area, just off Highway 50 and Antelope Valley Road. It wasn't much—just gravel, sagebrush, and sky—but it was shelter enough. We decided to wait out the storm there.

That evening, as lightning flashed to the east, headlights appeared through my window. A pickup slowed, turned in, and stopped near our camp. I slipped on my shoes and stepped out into the cooling air. Mr. T and Whiskey Tango were already talking with the driver—a rancher named Kevin, from the Hot Springs Ranch up Antelope Valley Road.

Kevin had seen our small convoy parked along the highway and decided to find out what we were all about. It didn't take long before we were deep in conversation. He was about my age—broad-shouldered, weathered, a man of the land. When he heard what the walk was about, the mission, and the letters we would carry for the people, something in him lit up.
"We've got to get our country back," he said. "These politicians are ruining everything that made it great."

We stood there in the glow of *Beechy's* porch light, talking about truth, responsibility, and how far the country had drifted. I told him what I told many others: "The problem isn't that truth is gone—it's that too many folks mistake opinions for truth. Truth's backed by facts, not by headlines or talking points."
Kevin nodded hard. "Amen to that," he said.

That night, the storm rolled east, but his words stayed with me.

The next morning, we returned to where we'd left off—about six miles back—and walked the stretch again to make it official. Most of the vehicles stayed parked at the pullout as we set out, planning to pick them up as we passed on the return. After that, Cindy and I continued on foot while the rest of the convoy—except *Beechy*—leapfrogged ahead toward our next stop, a paved parking area just west of the Eureka County Fairgrounds.

It felt good to be moving again, the air still cool and clean after the storm. We covered another five miles before calling it a day at a pullout near Devil's Gate. The red ridgelines cut sharply against the pale Nevada sky, and the scent of wet sage still hung in the air.

When we wrapped for the day, Cindy and I climbed into *Beechy* and rode the five or so miles to the paved parking area, where the rest of our crew had already set up camp. Later that afternoon, a long-haul trucker named Chris pulled in. He'd met my daughter in Reno and agreed to deliver a box of supplies she'd packed for us while hauling a load through to Colorado. He'd even timed his route just to meet up. We talked for a while, then shared dinner that evening at the Owl Restaurant before he hit the road again.

The following morning, we drove back to Devil's Gate to begin the next leg—walking from there back to the parking area. Not long after we arrived, a van pulled in and a man stepped out, camera gear in hand. He introduced himself as **Russ Varisco**, the creator of **RVerTV**, a YouTube channel that documents travel and life on the open road.

Russ had been driving back from Salt Lake City to Quartzsite, Arizona, filming along the way, when he heard about the Grey Wolf Walk and decided to track us down. We talked for a while—about the road, about freedom, and about the kind of people who still cross America with purpose rather than destination. He said he admired what we were doing—telling real stories, one step at a time, the way they used to be told: honest, unfiltered, and from the heart.

After a few still photos together, Russ unpacked his drone and asked if he could capture some aerial footage of the walk. We watched as it lifted into the bright Nevada sky, circling above the red ridges and the narrow stretch of Highway 50 below. In the wide shot, you could see all of us—Whiskey Tango, Miss Patty, Juniper, Texas Girl, Mr. T, Cindy, and me—standing together, waving up at the camera. For a few quiet moments, it felt like the whole journey had come into focus: the people, the purpose, and the long road still waiting ahead.

Before he left, I showed Russ the route we'd covered so far—the mile markers, the photos, and even some of the letters already in the Pony Express bag. He smiled and said, "That's the kind of story America needs to see."

The next day, the Eureka County Fair was in full swing—kids with cotton candy, music drifting through the fairgrounds, banners flapping in the desert wind. We handed out Grey Wolf Walk cards and talked with locals about the mission. Somewhere between the livestock pens and the food stalls, Texas Girl tapped my shoulder. "Sheriff's right behind you," she said.

I turned to see Sheriff **Jesse Watts**—a familiar face from an earlier chapter of the journey. I'd first met him back in May 2021 at a rally in Battle Mountain, where he and Sheriff **Ron Unger**, the Lander County Sheriff, spoke about constitutional law enforcement and the importance of standing firm on their oath. I'd followed their work even before that rally. As members of the Constitutional Sheriffs and Peace Officers Association, both men represented a rare breed—sheriffs who still stood unshaken by politics and rooted in principle.

We shook hands, and I told him how good it was to see him again.
"I've heard about you doing this walk," he said with a grin.
I laughed. "Then why didn't you come out and walk a mile with me from Devil's Gate?"
He shook his head. "Not in these cowboy boots, my friend."
"Trade them for tennis shoes," I said. "Just imagine the look on your deputies' faces if you walked back into town with me."
He chuckled. "No, I'm good."

We talked for a while about the challenges sheriffs face—how they answer to the people, not to politicians, yet still have to wrestle with county budgets and political pressure that try to pull the strings. We reminisced about that day in Battle Mountain, when he and Sheriff Unger spoke openly about the growing disconnect between government and the governed—and how vital it was for local law enforcement to remember who they serve. Both men understood the stakes then, and they still do now: how much authority—and how much responsibility—a principled sheriff holds in protecting the constitutional rights of the people.

After the fair, Sheriff Watts told us we could park at the welcome center just east of town. Officially, there was no overnight parking allowed—but he waved that off. "You've got my permission," he said. "You're fine."

The next morning, Miss Patty, Cindy, and I set out again from the parking area west of town. A light rain began to fall as we walked, the kind that softens the dust but never quite soaks through. We stopped for a short break at Rains Market before heading into downtown Eureka.

That's where I met Miss Dana, who ran the historical tours around town—especially of the "haunted" buildings that give Eureka its old Western charm. She was sharp, full of stories, and proud of her town. "You're doing a good thing," she told me. "Keep walking."

Miss Dana, Eureka County Tourism Director — August 2022

We also stopped at the old EZ Stop downtown, where two women behind the counter recognized me from my livestream. "You're the Grey Wolf guy!" one of them laughed. They signed the guest book, took some stickers, and promised to tell others about the walk. Their excitement spilled into the livestream chat, lifting everyone's spirits.

From there, I walked to the Sentinel Museum, where an old bell and a rusted safe from the 1800s stood out front. A small sign read: Ring the bell if you dare.

So I did—tapped it first with Wolfie, my walking stick, but it barely made a sound. Then I found the rope, gave it a hard pull, and the bell rang out clear and loud across the valley.

"Freedom!" I shouted, as the echo carried through town.

We ended that day's walk at the Chevron station in downtown Eureka, then moved to the welcome center that Sheriff Watts had approved for us. It was there we got word that Juniper and Texas Girl would have to head home. Juniper's employer needed him back in person, and though we'd hoped for more miles together, duty called. They had become like family on the road—our cooks, scouts, photographers, and motivators.

We also said goodbye to Cindy, who decided to continue her own route and explore independently. She'd been a spark of energy on the walk, and we wished her well as she rolled out that afternoon.

Before leaving, everyone pitched in to organize what we could. Juniper and Texas Girl helped pack supplies and arranged with the local fire department to store the overflow on a pallet inside an empty bay. Before pulling away, Texas Girl told me to keep their Starlink satellite unit so we could keep livestreaming. "Keep the light on," she said with a smile.

When they finally rolled east, the camp felt quieter. The reality set in —we no longer had a supply trailer. That meant no room for gear, tools, or extra fuel. My moderators and support team began calling around for solutions. Late that night, my daughter called.

"Dad," she said, "our neighbor Jerry just got a little six-by-eight trailer. He said you can use it as long as you need to."

The next morning, Whiskey Tango and Mr. T headed back to Reno to pick it up. While they were gone, I took *Beechy* into town to strengthen her towing setup. After a few conversations, I found Brown Brothers Fabrication, where Dan Brown welded steel reinforcements under the frame to make towing safe.

By the time Whiskey Tango and Mr. T returned, they'd not only picked up the trailer but also a temporary tag and an electric fan system to help keep Beechy's engine cool. Together, we spent two long days wiring lights, mounting gear, and getting everything road-ready.

The trailer wasn't fancy—just a weathered landscaper's hauler—but it was enough. We transferred the generator platform to the trailer tongue and organized our supplies like a small, mobile warehouse.

That night, as I looked over the freshly welded frame and the patched-up trailer, I realized how far we'd come since Austin. This walk was never meant to be about proving endurance—it was about connection. The wide, empty desert miles had been beautiful, but they hadn't brought people. I could talk to coyotes and cattle all day, but I needed to reach citizens.

The mission wasn't to walk every mile.
The mission was to awaken America.

So we made a new plan: drive the long, empty stretches and focus our walks on the towns—where the people were, where conversations could happen, where hearts could be moved.

I caught plenty of heat online from trolls claiming I'd broken my promise. But I hadn't. My promise was to carry the people's voices to Washington, not to count steps.

The road had changed, but the mission hadn't.
And with Beechy running stronger than ever, a new chapter of the *Grey Wolf Walk Across America for Freedom* was just beginning.

Chapter 31 – The Iron Road

We rolled out of Eureka later than planned, *Beechy* hitched to the new little trailer that would carry the rest of the Grey Wolf gear. The wind had shifted cooler, carrying the scent of wet sage from the storm that had passed through a few nights before. *Beechy* rumbled steady, but I could feel the strain in her old bones—fifty years of grit still clinging inside her cooling system the engine block and passages long overdue for a proper flush. Every uphill pull sent the temperature gauge creeping higher, and we'd have to ease over on the shoulder, letting her cool while the semis thundered past.

Between those stops, I started searching for answers—how to clean out a half-century of rust without tearing the motor apart on the side of Highway 50. Each mile east felt heavier, not just for *Beechy* but for all of us. The road from Eureka to Ely is long and barren, a stretch that tests patience and faith more than endurance.

When we finally reached the Love's Travel Center in Ely, the four of us—Mr. T, Whiskey Tango, Miss Patty, and me—were road-tired but grateful. We parked for the night and planned to drive back the next morning to a point five miles west of town to make the walk official, mile by mile. The idea was simple: walk into Ely, let people see the banners, the signs, the flag—maybe spark curiosity again.

The next morning, we did just that. Mr. T drove *Beechy* behind us while Whiskey Tango, Miss Patty, and I started down the shoulder toward town. The air was crisp, the sky high and blue, when I caught sight of something coming out of the canyon ahead—a thick plume of black smoke curling across the horizon.

At first, I thought it was a brush fire—until I heard it: the deep, rhythmic chuff of a steam locomotive.

Then came Mr. T's voice over the radio, half-singing, half-laughing:

"She'll be comin' 'round the mountain when she comes."

Out of the canyon thundered a magnificent machine—black iron gleaming, a wood tender hitched close behind—a living relic roaring back to life. It was one of the Nevada Northern Railway's engines, lovingly restored and run by volunteers who refused to let America's early heartbeat go silent.

Old No. 81.

I stopped right there on the shoulder and watched as the whistle blew—long and low, echoing across the valley. For a moment, it felt as if time folded, and the past came rolling forward to meet us.

Nevada Northern Railway No. 81 steam locomotive, Ely — August 2022

That engine wasn't just steel and steam; it was the sound of what built this country. I thought about the men who laid those rails, the sweat, the vision, the stubbornness to connect coast to coast. Without them, there would be no highways, no *Beechy*, no Grey Wolf Walk. We built this nation on courage like that—iron, fire, and belief. Seeing that locomotive roll past reminded me that even old engines, when cared for, can still climb the grades.

A little while earlier, before the train appeared, a white pickup had pulled up beside us. On the door, in black vinyl, were the words National Pony Express Association – Keeping the Legend Alive – Established 1978.

The driver was an elderly gentleman with kind eyes and calloused hands. He introduced himself and asked if we needed help—a question we heard often. People would see *Beechy* on the shoulder and assume she'd broken down. We laughed, shook hands, and I told him my walk was inspired by the spirit of the Pony Express riders—carrying letters of hope from Americans to the Capitol. His face lit up with a wide smile. "That's a fine idea," he said. "Keep the legend alive."

That encounter lingered in my mind even after he drove off and the locomotive thundered by. The past seemed to be walking with me that morning—horsemen, trainmen, truckers—all of them part of the same long story of Americans trying to move something forward.

We reached the first park in Ely—Veterans Memorial Park—and took a break, the steady hum of traffic blending with the rustle of flags overhead. Signs for the upcoming county fair hung on light poles, bright against the blue sky. We talked about heading there later, maybe mingling with the crowd to draw some attention to the walk. I couldn't help but hope the fair would bring a different kind of crowd—people ready to talk, maybe even to walk a few miles beside us.

But even as hope flickered, there was that quiet question in the back of my mind: Was anyone still listening?

Beechy cooled in the parking lot while the flags fluttered in the afternoon wind. Somewhere behind us, that old locomotive let out another whistle, and for a moment, the sound stretched across the desert like a memory refusing to fade.

Chapter 32 – The Silent Fair

The next morning, we returned to Veterans Memorial Park with hopes high and hearts steady. The plan was simple — set up at a table, hand out cards, and talk with anyone willing to listen. The grass was still wet from the sprinklers, and a light breeze carried the smell of grilled onions from a nearby food stand setting up for the day. But as the morning stretched on, the park stayed mostly quiet.

A few families wandered through, pausing to glance at the signs or snap photos of *Beechy* parked under the shade trees. One couple from the Elko area stopped to chat, walking a blue Frenchie that reminded me of Abby. Abby, of course, wanted to play, but their little dog hid behind their legs, shy and uncertain. We laughed, struck up a conversation, and before long I was explaining the Grey Wolf Walk and the Pony Express bag. They listened closely, nodded, and said, "You're doing a good thing." They signed the guest book and promised to send a letter for the Pony Express bag once they got home.

It wasn't the crowd we'd hoped for, but it was something. Every signature mattered. Every conversation counted.

Later that afternoon, Miss Patty and Whiskey Tango went exploring around town and ended up at the Nevada Northern Railway Museum. They came back wide-eyed, telling stories and showing photos of the great old locomotives—the smell of oil and steam still thick in the air, the engines standing like iron monuments to another era. Meanwhile, Mr. T and I handled the basics: laundry, cleaning, and reorganizing *Beechy*, making sure she'd be ready for the fair the next day. It felt good to restore a little order to the road-worn chaos. There's something grounding about folding clean clothes while the low hum of diesel fills the background.

The next day, we made our way to the county fairgrounds, hopeful for a larger crowd. The air buzzed with carnival music, kids darting between livestock pens and food stalls, lights beginning to flicker as the sun dropped behind the ridge. I carried a stack of walk cards and worked my way through the midway, explaining the walk and its purpose to anyone who paused long enough to listen.

Most people smiled politely, took a card, and moved on. But one woman, standing beside her husband near a corndog stand, looked down at the card, frowned, and handed it back.

"There's nothing wrong with this country," she said flatly. "You just have to vote and trust the system."

I smiled, thanked her for her time, and walked away. But her words followed me through the fairgrounds like an echo.

Trust the system?

I thought about how many people still believed everything would fix itself — that just showing up to vote was enough. Faith without awareness is a dangerous kind of sleep. Too many Americans had stopped asking questions. Too many were satisfied with answers handed to them in sound bites and headlines.

Back at *Beechy*, I told Mr. T about the encounter. He just shook his head. "That's why we're out here boss," he said quietly. "To wake a few more up."

The next morning, we packed up and left the Love's Travel Stop in Ely. I walked about five miles out of town with Whiskey Tango beside me while Mr T and Miss Patty drove behind us. We'd hoped a few locals might join us — maybe someone from the fair or the park — but no one did. Still, the road waited, and we walked.

The desert stretched out ahead—long, empty, and sun-bleached. Our next stop was Baker, Nevada, at the Utah border. The road climbed hard in places, and *Beechy's* temperature gauge climbed right along with it. More than once we had to pull over and let her cool down. Something had to be done; we couldn't keep tackling mountain passes with an engine that old and half-clogged with rust buildup.

By the time we rolled into Baker, the light had turned gold across the basin. We found a small RV park, set up camp, and sat outside to let the day unwind. Not far from us was a couple in a big diesel pusher, their rig gleaming in the sunset. They came over to chat, curious about *Beechy* and the walk, saying how much they wished they could join us—if only they weren't headed the opposite direction. Later, inside the bar near the restaurant, we met a cyclist from Colorado sitting at the counter. He was pedaling his way to California to raise awareness for cancer research. He insisted on buying us all dinner, and we shared the evening swapping stories—different roads, same determination.

Before leaving Baker the next morning, we got permission from the RV park owner to drain and flush *Beechy's* cooling system right there on-site. Rust-colored coolant poured out as we worked, clearing fifty-five years of buildup from her veins. When we finished, I started her up and listened—the hum was smoother now, the old girl breathing a little easier, but still not completely cleared.

In front, the Utah line ran right past the café and gas station where we'd spent the night. I started a livestream and walked across, Abby walking beside me. The border itself was simple—no fence, no gate—just a faded green sign and a change in the pavement. I stopped, planted my shoes on Utah soil, and looked back west toward Nevada.

"First border down," I said quietly. "Another promise kept."

Chapter 33 – Come Talk About Freedom

We drove on toward Delta, Utah, the road stretching flat and endless beneath a pale blue sky. The mountains fell away behind us, the land opening wide—fields, fences, and distant barns standing solitary against the horizon. *Beechy* still ran hot on the climbs, but she held together like an old mule with something left to prove.

By the time we rolled into Delta, the sun hung low and golden over the basin. We found a dirt lot along Highway 50, just down from the Tractor Supply store, and set up camp. A friendly sheriff's deputy stopped by, curious about our signs, and said it was fine for us to stay there a few days. That's when the next chapter of the walk began—one built not on miles but on conversations.

Whiskey Tango and I walked over to the auto-parts store on the west side of town to pick up the Thermocure we'd ordered while in Baker. When we got back, I started *Beechy* and listened to her hum—still running warm but steady and willing, ready for whatever came next.

We drained the old coolant and poured in the Thermocure, topping it off with plain water. The mixture gurgled through her lines as if clearing its throat after a long silence. The plan was to let it circulate for several days, loosening the rust and scale that had built up over half a century, then flush it out again down the road and replace it with fresh coolant. It wasn't perfect, but it was progress—and out here, that's what mattered most.

The next morning, as the town began to stir, a few travelers honked and waved from passing cars. I lifted Wolfie in salute, and Abby barked once as if to answer.

Using supplies we'd picked up at the local Tractor Supply, Mr. T, Whiskey Tango, and I set up a small table and an umbrella on the roadside beside the little trailer hitched behind *Beechy*.

It wasn't long before a white SUV pulled off the road and stopped near our camp. Out stepped a woman with a smile that matched the desert sun. She walked up, curious, and asked, "So what's this all about?"

Her name was Rayette. Within minutes we were deep in conversation about the state of the country, about hope, and about how one voice—multiplied by thousands—can still make a difference. She left and came back later with her husband, Dan, carrying a box, containing freeze-dried fruit and an assortment of vegetables, some eggs from their chickens, and a hand-woven tug toy for Abby. They stayed a while, talking about faith, family, and the road ahead. Before long, it felt like we'd known them for years. That's the kind of bond the road makes—short meetings that linger like family.

Rayette told us she wanted to help however she could. She made a handmade sign that read "Come Talk About Freedom" and brought it to us later that afternoon. We taped it to our little table and umbrella by *Beechy*—our new Freedom Table. On it sat our guest book, walk cards, and the Grey Wolf Pony Express bag, open for letters.

Beechy and the Freedom Table, Delta, Utah — August 2022.

Whiskey Tango paired his phone to a Bluetooth speaker, and soon **Steve Spurgeon's** *"Wake Up in the USA"* drifted across Main Street. The lyrics carried like a prayer through the warm Delta air:

"There's a cry of freedom sweepin' around the world today,

Here we have it all—life and liberty. Still, we give the dream away.

No more can we afford to stand around, set aside our ways.

Wake up in the USA. Wake up in the USA."

I smiled, remembering the call I'd had with Steve months earlier, when he gave me permission to use his song as the theme for the walk. "Just make sure people really listen to the words," he'd told me. That day, hearing it echo across Delta, I knew they were.

Not long after, a few locals stopped to chat—Travis and Trevor, brothers who'd seen us online. They signed the guest book and promised to spread the word about the community walk we were planning for the weekend. Dan returned later that evening and sat with us for a couple of hours. We talked about what freedom means now, and how too many people have forgotten that it starts with courage, not comfort. "They can't cancel you if you stand together," he said. I nodded, knowing he was right.

As the day faded into dusk, the town lights flickered on. The air cooled, and the sky deepened to that soft indigo only the desert knows. Abby curled up beside my chair, worn out from greeting everyone who stopped by. *Beechy* idled quietly behind us, her old engine ticking as it cooled. Across the road, headlights came and went, but a sense of calm lingered.

The next morning, Dan dropped Rayette off again—flag in hand, ready to walk. Miss Patty joined us for a short two-mile stretch that began just west of town and wound up on Delta's Main Street. The walk wasn't long, but it was powerful. Drivers honked and waved, a few rolled down their windows to shout encouragement. One woman even pulled over just to say, "Keep going—we need this!"

About halfway through town, I spotted a man standing off to the side with a large telephoto lens. He turned out to be a photographer for the Millard County Chronicle Progress, who'd heard about the Grey Wolf Walk and wanted to capture the moment. We spoke briefly as he snapped a few photos of us walking under the "Welcome to Delta" sign. Later, he told me the paper would be running a feature and that the story was already up on their Facebook page.

When we finished our walk, we circled back to the Freedom Table. Abby drank from her bowl while Rayette laughed, saying, "You'd think we'd just marched across the whole state." In a way, we had. Each step was a statement, each mile a message: the people still cared.

That afternoon, Sam Jacobson, the reporter from the Chronicle, stopped by to follow up on the story. We talked about the purpose behind the walk—how it wasn't about endurance but about awakening people to their own voices again. He nodded and said, "You're doing something folks need right now. You're reminding them they still count."

As the day wound down, I looked around our little camp—*Beechy*, the trailer, the table, the sign. Simple things, but together they stood for something larger. Rayette and Dan waved goodbye, promising to return in the morning. The street quieted, and a warm glow hung over the horizon.

That night, as the desert cooled and the stars came alive, I sat outside *Beechy* and thought about how far we'd come since Eureka. This chapter of the walk wasn't about distance—it was about connection. For the first time in a long while, it felt like the message was landing. People were listening again.

Tomorrow we'd pack up and move toward Payson, bringing the conversation with us. The road ahead would be long, but the fire was still burning bright.

The walk was changing shape, but not its heart.

We were still out here—one step, one town, one voice at a time.

Chapter 34 – Different Flags, Same Fight

Morning came soft and gold over Delta, the kind of light that makes even the dust shine. Abby stretched beside *Beechy's* front tire while Mr. T and Whiskey Tango packed up the Freedom Table and folded the umbrella. Across the lot, a lifted Jeep rolled in—Dan and Rayette, come to see us off one more time.

Rayette hopped out holding a thermos of coffee and some homemade breakfast for us, her smile as bright as ever. Dan shook my hand hard, then set his other hand on my shoulder.
"If anyone gives you trouble," he said, looking me dead in the eye, "you let me know—anywhere in this country—and I'll come help you out, wherever you need it."

I felt that promise deep in my chest. It wasn't just talk; it was the kind of vow only an American with calloused hands and a clean conscience can make. We took a quick photo together beside *Beechy*, Abby between us. When they drove off, Rayette waved out the window until they disappeared around the corner.

We turned east onto Highway 6, leaving the basin behind. The land rolled gently now—open, dry, framed by low ridges. *Beechy* hummed steady behind us, towing the little trailer and the miles of stories we'd gathered since Nevada.

By late morning we rolled into Payson, the sun already high and fierce. We pulled into a small city park where Texas Girl—one of our ever-reliable supporters on Discord—had said she'd spoken with someone from the city and gotten permission for us to stay the night.

But about an hour or so later, a pair of police cruisers eased up beside *Beechy*. The officers were polite but firm. After I explained that one of our team had cleared it with a city employee, they nodded, then shook their heads.
"Sorry," one said, "you can't stay here overnight. Walmart's your best bet."

So we packed everything back up, fired up *Beechy*, and rolled to the south side of town, parking near the auto-center side of the Walmart lot. A supporter had called ahead and ordered a small barbecue grill, so we went inside, picked it up along with some fresh chicken, and fired it up right there beside *Beechy*.

It wasn't long before the smell drifted across the lot. Mechanics and technicians from the Auto Center began stepping out to the edge of their bays, sniffing the air and grinning. I wrapped a few pieces of chicken in foil and walked them over, explaining what the Grey Wolf Walk was all about. They were grateful—and when they closed up for the night, each of them honked their horn as they drove past, waving out their windows.

The next morning, Miss Patty joined me for the walk out of Payson toward Salem. Mr. T followed behind in *Beechy*, with Whiskey Tango trailing him, while we set off on foot. The day warmed quickly, the air sharp and bright, until the quiet was broken by a sudden chorus of barking—dozens of dogs echoing across the valley. We looked over to see a sprawling kennel off to our right, rows of chain-link and wagging tails. Some barked warnings; others just wanted to be part of something moving past.

Miss Patty laughed. "Guess we woke up the whole neighborhood," she said.

We walked on, shoes crunching the gravel shoulder. A few drivers offered freedom honks, each one lifting our spirits a little higher. Then a gentleman pulled over ahead of us, rolled down his passenger window, and called out, "What are you doing out here?" He'd noticed the signs on the backs of our vehicles. I walked up and told him briefly about the walk—what it stood for, what we were trying to do. He reached into his pocket, pulled out a fifty-dollar bill, and handed it to me.

"Keep up the good work," he said, smiling as he honked and waved before driving off.

We picked up our pace again, grinning like kids who'd just been reminded the world still held good people.

By late morning we reached the edge of Salem, Utah—a small town stitched together with tidy homes, white fences, and the steady hum of school life. Then, just outside a gym called Total Fitness, a couple stepped out to watch us pass. They'd seen the signs and the old RV trailing behind.

"Hey, what's this all about?" one of them called out.

I entered the lot to shake their hands and told them the truth—that it wasn't about politics or parties, but about remembering who we are. About citizens relearning that they hold the reins of this republic. They nodded, eyes softening as the meaning sank in.

"Man, that's pretty cool," one said. "You don't see stuff like this anymore."

Miss Patty switched places with Whiskey Tango, and a little way ahead, a group of high-school kids were walking back toward campus after lunch. They'd spotted the sign on the back of Miss Patty's trailer— "Honk's 4 Freedom"—with the words about the walk printed just below it.

They turned, smiling, and started cheering. One boy pumped his arm in the air, signaling for drivers to honk, and before long the whole street came alive with sound—horns blaring, kids laughing, flags waving from passing cars.

For a few blocks it felt like a parade. They didn't know me, but in that moment, we were walking together. Hope can be contagious like that.

When they finally turned up the road toward the school, Whiskey Tango and I pressed on past the edge of town. I caught myself smiling at a simple realization: not a single one of those kids had their face buried in a cell phone. They were just walking, talking—living in the moment. Something you don't see much anymore.

By the time we reached the north side of town, *Beechy* was overdue for her flush and oil change. We pulled into Oil Rig Automotive, a small lube shop with a sun-faded sign. The guys there were friendly—one even recognized *Beechy* from the paper. They waved us in and said we could use their bay.

The three of us got to work draining the Thermocure. Rusty water poured out like the past leaving her veins. We replaced the filters, filled her with fresh oil, refilled the radiator with clean coolant, and hit every grease point while we were at it. When I turned the key and she rumbled back to life, the idle was smoother, the temp gauge steadier. She was old—but she was healing.

As we were cleaning up, my phone buzzed. Unknown number—Canada.

It was James Topp, the Canadian veteran walking across his country at the same time I was crossing ours. Our supporters had been trying to connect us for weeks, and now we were finally talking—two soldiers on two long roads, walking for freedom in two nations that seemed to have lost their way.

James's voice carried the same mix of fatigue and conviction I felt in my own bones. His mission was to bring attention to vaccine mandates and government overreach affecting Canada's military and workers. Mine, though parallel, reached deeper into the soul—to remind Americans of their responsibility to guard liberty itself.

We talked for nearly half an hour—about endurance, about faith, and about how both our walks had become more spiritual than political. Before we ended the call, we agreed to hold a live-stream panel together on September 6 at 10 a.m. Pacific. Since we both had Starlink systems, we could even walk and talk at the same time—two men on different roads, sharing one mission.
"Talk to you on the sixth," I said.

When the line went quiet, I sat in *Beechy's* driver's seat for a long moment, listening to her engine purr. Two veterans. Two flags. One purpose.

We gave the shop a little money for letting us use their bay and pulled *Beechy* out, moving her across the street to the county parking lot where we'd spend the night. Evening was settling in by the time we wrapped up. The three of us crossed over to Main Street Pizza, stomachs growling after a long day. The place smelled like heaven—dough, garlic, and wood smoke mingling in the air.

Whiskey Tango ordered for all of us, counting out bills and coins at the counter. The young man behind the register froze, confused when Whiskey Tango handed him extra change so the return would come out even. We stood there watching as the kid tried to make sense of it, tapping buttons on the screen until the register told him what to do.

We just smiled. The world had changed since we were young—math used to come from the head, not a computer—but we weren't laughing at him. It was just one of those quiet reminders of how much the old ways had faded.

We couldn't help but chuckle as the kid struggled. "I just wanted a five back," Whiskey Tango said, grinning.

"I can't do it without the computer," the cashier admitted, turning red. We shook our heads good-naturedly, joking that maybe that was what had gone wrong with America—we'd forgotten how to count back change.

While we waited for the pizzas, we talked about the day—the kids in Salem, the gym couple, James Topp's call, Beechy's flush. When the pies came out hot and bubbling, we carried them across the road to the county yard where Miss Patty was holding down our camp. The sun was sinking low, painting the sky in deep oranges and pinks.

We ate sitting in camp chairs beside *Beechy*, the first stars blinking awake overhead. Abby wandered from one of us to the next, hoping for pizza bones. Across the lot, the old rig gleamed faintly under a single pole light, her cooling system finally clear, her heart steady again.

It had been a day of work, laughter, and meaning—the kind that reminds you why you started.

As the desert night folded around us, I thought of the people we'd met—Dan and Rayette's promise, the kids waving, the couple at the gym, James Topp's voice echoing down a different road. Different flags, same fight.

Freedom was still alive—carried in every handshake, every honk, every step.

Chapter 35 – Spanish Fork (A Stirring in the Spirit)

We left the county parking lot in Salem just after sunrise. The air was already warm, the light cutting sharp across the pavement. Miss Patty and I walked the stretch out of town while Mr. T and Whiskey Tango followed in the rigs. The shoulder sloped gently upward, fields on either side, the hum of the highway steady and low. Every few minutes I'd look back and see *Beechy* in the early light, that familiar silhouette rolling slow and steady like an old friend who knew the road by heart.

A few miles in, on the right, a small restoration shop caught my eye. The yard was lined with American steel—late-'50s Fords, early-'60s Falcon, a '63 Buick Special, a '60 Studebaker, and a Chrysler 300 sitting half in the open garage, its chrome flashing like a mirror to another time. For a while we just walked in silence, both of us admiring the kind of craftsmanship that once defined this country. Detroit grit. Cars built to last—simple, honest, fixable. I couldn't help but think of *Beechy*: a '67 Beechwood motorhome on a Dodge P300 chassis. Same soul. Same stubborn will to keep going.

A mile or so later, near the edge of South Spanish Fork, an old horse-drawn wagon stood out front of a business—a relic from the 1800s, wood gray and weathered, iron-clad wheels still proud. It sat like a monument to endurance. Seeing it in the heat of that morning, I thought, *That's America right there*—the will to keep moving, no matter how heavy the load.

By early afternoon, the temperature had climbed past a hundred. We ended the walk on a patch of pavement in the parking lot of the Russell Swenson Baseball Complex, near a building that belonged to a business next door. We parked *Beechy* with Whiskey Tango and Miss Patty's rig tucked close behind, angling both to catch the thin stretch of shade cast by that building. Abby stretched out near the steps, tongue lolling, content just to be still. The shade didn't move much, but we moved with it—chairs scooting a foot or two every forty-five minutes like a sundial that refused to give up.

Those first two days in Spanish Fork felt like an intermission. We washed clothes in a downtown laundromat that smelled like soap and hot metal, rinsed dust off the folding table, wiped down the inside of

Beechy. I tightened a loose clamp on the heater hose and checked the belts. You never fully rest on the road; you just change the kind of work you're doing.

Folks wandered over, curious about the flags and the signs. One older gentleman in a John Deere hat set two cold waters on our table, tapped the bill of his cap, and said, "Appreciate what you're doin', son," then shuffled back to his pickup without waiting for a thank-you. A mom with two kids brought a bag of ice and asked what time we usually started walking. "Early," I said. "Before the heat finds us." She laughed and said the heat always finds you in August.

On the second day, Miss Rayette pulled in from Delta. She'd come up for her grandkids' school event and made time to find us. She stepped out smiling, carrying a box of freeze-dried fruit, fresh vegetables, some homemade roasted chicken, and a big watermelon—one of the orange-fleshed kinds you don't see often anymore. "You've got to stay fueled," she said, handing them over. The food smelled like home—simple, honest, made with care. She gave us each a hug, waved, and promised she'd be back again. With Rayette, "I'll be back" always meant soon.

That morning's walk livestream ran from the moment my shoes hit the shoulder. The chat filled quickly—supporters, newcomers, and, of course, a handful of trolls who thought they could steer a moving train with a few keystrokes. One of them typed, "The convoy did more than this walk ever will."

I didn't miss a step. *"Trucks make noise,"* I said, *"but people make change."*

The feed went quiet. Then the honest questions started rolling in: What does change look like? Why walk and not rally? I talked about what separated noise from movement. You can line up three hundred trucks and it looks powerful—but thousands of people walking shoulder to shoulder? That's what wakes a nation up. This was never about horsepower. It was about heart.

A few called me lazy. I laughed. *"Come walk a mile with me,"* I told them. *"Then tell me about lazy."* Someone wrote, I could do ten easy. I said, *"Meet me at mile marker 3 and we'll find out."* The chat sent laughing emojis and prayer hands. It wasn't an endurance test—it was a call to conscience. The measure wasn't miles; it was conversations.

After a couple of nights at Russell Swenson, we packed up and moved to the Love's Truck Stop on the north side of town. Something about Spanish Fork tugged at me. I couldn't explain it—just this steady sense that we needed to stay a little longer. A whisper in the back of my mind kept saying, Spanish Fork matters. Sometimes the road speaks in sentences. Sometimes it's just a tug in your chest you can't ignore.

Love's hummed with the constant life of the highway—reefers chugging, air tools whining, the metallic bark of a fifth-wheel locking home. Our little camp slotted into that rhythm. We set the table, straightened the banner, refilled Abby's bowl. The sun rode high, and the smell of diesel and warm rubber became the backdrop to our days.

Once we'd set up camp, Whiskey Tango and I drove up to Salt Lake City to collect burlap sacks that one of my supporters had secured from a company there—rough and plain, the kind you'd once see filled with grain or coffee beans. We didn't have overflow yet, but I hoped we soon would. The sacks were a kind of faith in what was coming—preparation for the day when the Grey Wolf Pony Express bag would no longer be enough to hold all the letters and cards people were sending. Each note would represent a voice—a prayer, a protest, a promise. Every one of them would matter. And when the time came, we'd carry them all the way to Washington, D.C.

On the drive back down I-15, we talked logistics—how to catalog the letters, how to keep water cold without burning through ice, how well the livestream worked with the Starlink system as long as Mr. T didn't get to far away with *Beechy*. It's the unglamorous details that make a mission real. At a red light, Whiskey Tango looked over and said, "You think folks will fill these?" I patted the stack of burlap on the floorboard. *"I think they already have. They just don't know it yet."*

The day after we returned, Rayette came back, keeping her word. This time she carried something different: a copy of the Millard County Chronicle Progress, the issue that ran our Delta story. She handed it to me like a gift from home. "Thought you'd want a keepsake," she said. I ran my hand over the print, the smell of ink mixing with diesel fumes. It wasn't fame—it was proof that our message had legs.

That same afternoon, I teased a surprise on the livestream—told the viewers something big was coming. I was sitting inside *Beechy*, giving a daily update, when Mr. T stuck his head in and said, "You've got a visitor out back."

Out behind *Beechy*, we'd set up a small table and grill, the afternoon light slanting across the lot. I grabbed my livestream camera and stepped outside, still talking to the audience, drawing it out—keeping them guessing. I kept the lens close to my chest so the chat could only see sky and the top of the umbrella, and the comments started flying: What is it? Who's there? Don't do us like this, Grey Wolf!

Then, as I rounded the corner, I panned the camera wide and revealed the surprise.

There he was—Gypsy.

He'd taken a Greyhound bus into Provo and walked to the Love's truck stop to find us. The convoy's cook, the heart and backbone of its second half, stood there with that big grin and road dust on his shoes. He lifted a hand like he was greeting an old classmate, looked straight into the lens, and said, "Heard the Grey Wolf needed some miles covered."

The chat exploded. GYPSY!!! Chef's in the house! Let's goooo! He waved at the camera, then told my viewers, in his own words, why he'd come—to walk beside me, to carry the message forward, to keep the flame of freedom burning one step at a time. *"Convoy or walk, same heartbeat,"* he said. *"We feed people, then we lead people."*

Seeing him made me feel good inside. He'd been a brother on the road during the convoy's long return from Hagerstown. Now he'd come to walk beside me for a while. But his arrival also marked change—within days I'd be saying goodbye to Whiskey Tango and Miss Patty. That's the math of the road: every hello counts down to a goodbye. You learn to hold both at once.

We fired up the little grill as the sun lowered, laid on a couple of chicken breasts and pork chops, and talked plans. Abby sat like a statue, eyes hopeful for an Abby bite. A mechanic from the shop across the way drifted over with a "What y'all cooking?" and left with a foil packet and a smile. Truckers honked as they rolled past, that language we all speak without words.

Gypsy wanted to stretch his legs, so we hit the road together the next morning for a walk to town and back. He wore a small pack and that near-constant half-smile that says I'm where I'm supposed to be. We traded stories—convoy memories, roadside meals, the little things that kept us human. He admitted he'd underestimated the walk. "You're a machine, old man," he laughed. I grinned. *Just stubborn.* He told me how in some towns feeding people was like lighting a fuse—he'd watch a plate turn into a conversation, and a conversation into a small rally right there in the parking lot. We didn't need blueprints. We needed neighbors.

That evening brought something special—a long-awaited livestream with James Topp, the Canadian veteran walking across his own country. Our moderators had spent weeks trying to sync schedules, and at last, everything lined up. I tested the Starlink system mounted on *Beechy's* mirror, checked the battery levels, and wiped the phone lens with the corner of my shirt like it was church china. When showtime came, the signal locked in—green lights across the board.

James connected through his Starlink, camera bouncing slightly as he walked some remote Canadian highway. You could hear the metronome of his stride in the audio. I sat inside *Beechy* at the dinette, headset on, ready to talk. Viewers on both sides of the border tuned in, comments flying like confetti and Scripture verses.

James spoke first, explaining his mission—to stand against government mandates that stripped Canadians of choice. Soldiers like him were being forced to take the shot or lose their careers. He walked for their freedom. He didn't raise his voice. He didn't need to. The steadiness did the lifting.

When it was my turn, I said, *"Our causes are different only by flag. We're both walking to remind people of the same truth—that freedom is a birthright, not a permission slip."* I talked about the 1948 Nuremberg Code, the promise of informed consent written after the darkest days of history. *"No government has the moral right to dictate what goes into your body or your soul,"* I said. *"Not in Ottawa. Not in Washington."*

Questions poured in. How do I get involved without getting fired? What do I say to my kids? What's the first step if I'm scared? We answered the way the road had taught us to answer: start small, stand with someone, speak simply. Find your county meeting. Read your Constitution. Shake your neighbor's hand, even if he voted different. Courage isn't loud; it's consistent.

For nearly an hour—two veterans, two flags, one purpose—we walked and talked. The chat lit up with encouragement: Stand tall. Keep walking. We're with you. Someone typed, I thought I was alone. Another replied, You're not. You could feel the spirit rising through the screens, the way a crowd stands before the anthem without anyone asking it to.

We closed with a quiet promise—keep going. He on his road, me on mine. If we crossed paths again, good. If not, the work would still meet in the middle.

When the stream ended, I sat in the soft hum of *Beechy's* cabin, the generator running steady in the background. Outside, trucks idled low and rhythmic, their red tail-lights pulsing against the base of the mountains. Abby climbed onto the dinette seat beside me and rested her chin on my leg, like she'd been listening the whole time. That voice came back—quiet but certain: *Spanish Fork matters.*

Maybe it was because Rayette had driven hours just to bring a newspaper and say she believed. Maybe it was because Gypsy had shown up wearing worn-out shoes, ready to walk. Maybe it was because James Topp and I had finally joined hands across a continent, proving the road is wider than any one map.

The next afternoon, between errands and a short walk, I set up the livestream from outside Beechy. The rumble of diesel engines rolled through the lot like distant thunder. A truck driver had been watching from a few spaces over, leaning on his rig's fender, eyes fixed on the flags and the signs. Eventually, curiosity got the better of him, and he wandered over.

"What's all this about?" he asked, nodding toward the Grey Wolf banner.

I told him the truth—that I was walking for faith, freedom, and the soul of America. That it wasn't about politics or parties, but about remembering who we are and what was written to guide us. I reached inside *Beechy* and pulled out one of the small pocket Constitutions that supporters had mailed to me—a whole box of them to hand out along the way.

"Ever read this?" I asked, flipping it open to the second paragraph of the Declaration of Independence.
He shook his head. "Not since high school."

I read it aloud—the part about governments deriving *"their just powers from the consent of the governed."* He stood there a long moment, the sound of the idling semis filling the silence. Then he nodded slowly, eyes narrowing with thought.
"So," he said, "we're the boss?"

"Exactly," I told him. *"But only if we act like it."*

He took the booklet and ran a calloused thumb across the seal before slipping it into his shirt pocket. "Thanks," he said quietly, then turned and climbed back into his truck.

Moments like that were why I walked. Not for headlines or crowds, but for the chance to remind one person at a time what freedom really means.

Maybe that's why Spanish Fork mattered. Not the size of the town. Not the number of horns or the views on the stream. It was the alignment. The heart, the message, the mission—click, click, click—falling into place like a ratchet on a bolt you finally got square.

In the evenings the wind would ride down off the Wasatch and cool the lot just enough to make coffee sound like a good idea again. We'd sit in our camp chairs and plan our walk out of town, tracing highway 6 with a fingertip, checking shoulders and intersections on the map app. Mr. T jotted fuel stops. Gypsy circled a couple of markets where he figured we could stretch dollars into meals.

The plan was simple: keep moving east. Keep finding people. Keep turning noise into movement.

In a day or so, we'd say goodbye to Whiskey Tango and Miss Patty and roll out again, bound for the next town that needed reminding. But that night, under the pole light and a sky salted with early stars, I thought about how God often hides the turning points in plain places— truck stops and ballfield lots, grocery store aisles and quiet conversations with folks just trying to understand how their country works.

Spanish Fork wasn't a headline. It was a hinge.

When I finally crawled into *Beechy*, I could still hear the rhythm of the day—the steady hum of the generator running, Gypsy's soft laugh rolling from one story into the next, Miss Patty humming a tune she probably didn't realize she was humming. I propped the Chronicle Progress on the counter so it'd be the first thing I saw in the morning. Proof. Not of me. *Of us.*

Freedom wasn't a slogan anymore. It was alive—carried in every handshake, every mile, every person brave enough to stand.

And that was enough to keep me walking.

Chapter 36 – Fading Echoes

The next morning, we said our goodbyes to Whiskey Tango and Miss Patty—tearful hugs before parting ways. A family emergency had called them away, and though we all understood, the space they left behind felt heavier than expected.

Then we rolled east out of Spanish Fork, into a different kind of silence—one that didn't come from the desert, but from within. I still started every morning the same way: coffee in *Beechy's* tiny kitchen, a quiet prayer, the stretch of road unfolding like a promise I intended to keep. But somewhere past the city limits, I began to notice fewer names in the livestream chat. The familiar faces—the screen names that had cheered me through storms and climbs—were thinning out like a crowd after the fireworks fade. The counter that had once showed thousands, now hovered in the double digits, occasionally flickering back over two hundred before fading again.

I told myself it was just timing—people busy with life, or maybe the algorithms working against me again. But the truth pressed in. The spark that had drawn so many early on was fading. I was still walking, still waving that flag, still stopping to talk with anyone who would listen—still believing. But the world had already moved on to the next headline.

Gypsy and I walked out of Spanish Fork hoping others might join us as we made our way through town toward Highway 6—but no one did. When the miles gave way to open road, we climbed back aboard *Beechy* on the edge of town and set out for Duchesne City.

The ascent up Highway 191 was brutal. It pushed *Beechy* to her limit—engine straining, the trailer tugging hard against her frame. Her cooling system held steady, but that climb was beyond what she was built for. Still, she made it.

We spent the night at a small truck stop west of town. From there eastward, every place seemed a little smaller than the last—Duchesne, Roosevelt, Vernal—each with just a few stoplights and a church steeple reaching higher than anything else.

I started to have shoulder pain by then—a deep, grinding ache in my left arm that wouldn't ease. I told myself it was just strain from the pack, a tendon pulled from repetition. I'd walked off worse. But even as I said it, I knew something was different. My arm had started to stiffen, and I found myself cradling it close like a broken wing.

From Duchesne we pushed east into Roosevelt. The livestream was on, but the road was quiet. The land stretched out flat and open—miles of farmland broken by weathered barns and rusted tractors sitting idle in the sun. Cattle stood motionless in the heat, tails flicking at flies.

Beechy followed behind me now, steady and alone, her engine's hum the only sound breaking the silence as I walked through each small town —still waving the flag, still believing someone might step out and join.

In Roosevelt, we spent one night parked at a small Pilot station and the next at a park in town. I remember watching a few people playing something they called frisbee golf. I had to laugh—I'd never heard of the sport before. The sight of them walking the course with discs instead of clubs felt oddly fitting for this stretch of the journey— familiar, but somehow new.

While we were at the park, I called an old acquaintance—**Duane Olinger**, the owner of *Blind Frog Ranch*. We'd met months earlier during the Convoy at Russell's Truck Stop in New Mexico. He'd been curious then, supportive—one of those men who carries the spirit of old America in his handshake.

"Where you at, brother?" he asked when he picked up.
"Coming through Roosevelt. Heading your direction," I told him.
Duane was back home near Amarillo, Texas, but he didn't hesitate. "You stay in the parking lot at the outpost there in Vernal," he said. "You can use it for a few days. I'll tell the boys to expect you."
And that was that.

The *Blind Frog Ranch Outpost* sat on a corner in Vernal—a wide dirt lot beside an old storefront, wrapped in a kind of stillness that settled deep in your bones. We parked *Beechy* on the edge of the lot, set up the 10×10 flag-designed canopy one of my supporters had sent, unfolded the table, hung the Grey Wolf banner across *Beechy's* front, and built our little post on the frontier once again.

Ron "Grey Wolf" Coleman with Charlie from the Blind Frog Ranch Outpost, Vernal, UT. — September 2022

That afternoon, **Matt Wilber** from the local radio station, **KVEL (AM 920)**, stopped by to talk. We stood in the shade beside *Beechy*, the heat rising off the dirt lot, and I told him what the walk was about—the purpose, the message, the miles behind it. He listened with that calm, curious look you see in people who still believe words matter.

Later that evening, a pickup truck rolled into the lot and slowed beside us. The driver, a man named **Steve Evans**, leaned out the window and introduced himself as the station's owner. "Heard you've been stirring things up," he said with a grin. "How about coming by the station tomorrow morning for an interview—say, nine o'clock?" I agreed without hesitation.

The next morning, I walked the miles out to the station on the north side of town. When I stepped inside, Steve wasn't there yet, so I waited in the small lobby, listening to **Glenn Beck** and a few other voices coming through the monitor speaker behind the receptionist's desk. A few minutes later, the door opened and Steve came in.

"Where's your vehicle?" he asked.

"I walked." I said with a grin.

His eyes went wide. "You walked? Damn, you should've said something —I'd have swung by to give you a ride!"

I laughed and told him I was used to walking.

We stepped into a vacant sound booth, the faint hum of the equipment filling the silence as Steve adjusted the mic levels. He hit record and leaned forward with a grin.

"Ron, we've got folks asking about the flag and that old RV in town," he said. "What's the mission?"

I leaned against the desk, and spoke into the mic.

"I'm walking from Carson City, Nevada, all the way to our nation's capital," I said. *"Hoping to have that Forrest Gump moment—people joining along the way, not for me, but for what this country stands for."*

I paused, letting the hum of the equipment fill the silence before continuing.

"It's about reminding people of what they already know—that this country was built by ordinary folks willing to do extraordinary things. And that freedom isn't something we inherit once; it's something we have to keep alive."

He went quiet for a moment, eyes fixed on the console. Then he said softly, "You know, that sounds like something we used to say around here. Maybe folks just forgot."

He asked a few more questions—about the walk, the flag, the people I'd met along the way—and I answered them all. By the time we wrapped, he was nodding along with every word. He turned toward the mic and said to his listeners, "If you're curious, stop by the Blind Frog Ranch Outpost and meet Ron 'Grey Wolf' yourself. He's the real deal."

A moment later, his mother stepped into the room—sweet lady, proud as could be. She asked if she could take a few pictures of me and Steve for the station's page, then used my phone to snap the same ones so I'd have copies too. When we finished, Steve offered me a ride back to the lot, and we talked the whole way—about the walk, the country, and how sometimes it takes a few miles to wake people up again.

The interview ran that afternoon. Within a few hours, cars began pulling into the lot—slow, curious, windows rolling down. Folks wanted

Ron "Grey Wolf" Coleman with Steve Evans at KVEL (AM920), Vernal, UT. — September 2022

to see for themselves what the walk was about. Some took selfies beside *Beechy*; others asked questions, shook my hand, and signed the Grey Wolf Walk guestbook. The air buzzed with that small-town kind of energy—genuine curiosity mixed with quiet respect.

They came one or two at a time—a retired couple in a sun-faded Buick, a young mom with her boy, maybe twelve, and a man in oil-field coveralls who parked across the lot and just listened for a while before stepping forward.

Most had heard the radio broadcast. Some had caught the livestream. A few had no idea exactly what they were seeing—they just knew it looked like America.

I handed out walk cards and pocket Constitutions, each one feeling like a seed tossed into dry ground. Some smiled, took photos, shook hands. Others shared their stories—job losses, mandates, division, the feeling that the country they loved had slipped into something unrecognizable. I listened more than I spoke.

By sunset, there were maybe a dozen new names in the guestbook, each one written in careful pen strokes, as if the act itself mattered more than whatever came next.

That night, the desert cooled fast. The stars rose sharp over the outpost, and the hum of *Beechy's* generator filled the spaces where the crowd used to be. The season was shifting from summer to fall—we had left Spanish Fork on the first day of September, and you could feel the change coming. I sat under the canopy with a notebook and wrote a few lines that would never make it to the livestream:

Maybe the walk isn't about how many join, but how many wake up.
Maybe the sound of freedom isn't the roar of a convoy, but the steady steps of a single believer refusing to stop.

We spent a few more days there while waiting on some items that were being shipped to me. Each morning, I fired up the livestream. The chat still filled—but not like before. Twenty people, maybe thirty, sometimes close to a hundred. A few faithful supporters, some new faces, and the inevitable trolls—always there to stir the pot.

One wrote, "Where's your army now, Wolf? Looks like it's just you and a busted-up RV."
I smiled into the camera. *"Sometimes an army starts with one."*

Another chimed in, "You're wasting your time. Nobody cares anymore."
I leaned closer to the mic. *"Then maybe it's my job to remind them why they should."*

The chat went quiet.
It's funny how silence online feels louder than silence in person. You can almost sense people thinking—fingers paused above the keyboard, hearts deciding which way to lean.

Once the deliveries arrived, we secured everything for our last night there. The next morning, Gypsy and I packed up and walked out of town, *Beechy* rolling close behind. We stopped long enough to take photos at the veterans' memorial, then pushed on a bit farther before boarding her again on the outskirts and heading east toward the next stop. My shoulder ached worse with every mile, the pain deepening like a storm front moving in. By the time we crossed into Colorado, my left arm was nearly useless.

The livestreams had dwindled to maybe fifty to seventy viewers at a time, but I still went live every day—habit, duty, faith. I'd start with the sunrise, letting the light spill across the asphalt as I walked, then talk about whatever the day gave me—an old barn, a passing hawk, the memory of someone I'd met a hundred miles back.

Somewhere before Fort Collins, I caught myself humming "Wake Up in the USA" under my breath—the same song **Steve Spurgeon** had written months earlier, the one that had become the anthem of the walk. The lyrics hit differently now. Back then, it was a rallying cry. Now it felt like a prayer whispered into the wind.

"No more can we afford to stand around, set aside our ways. Wake up in the USA."

The highway carried me forward, but part of me wanted to turn around—to see if anyone was still following. I didn't. You can't walk by faith and keep looking backward.

When we finally reached the Colorado line, we pulled *Beechy* to the shoulder and climbed out. The sky stretched forever, blue and unforgiving. My left arm hung limp at my side, the sling cutting into my neck. I raised my right hand and saluted the flag mounted to the back of the trailer.

"Still walking," I whispered.

Behind me, the road shimmered in the fading heat. Ahead, it vanished into distance.

Mr. T came up beside me. "You all right, boss?"

"Yeah," I lied.

He looked at my shoulder. "You sure?"

"Not really," I admitted.

He nodded slowly.

"Then we keep going 'til you can't." I smiled. *"That's the plan."*

We climbed back in, *Beechy's* old engine grumbling to life, the smell of oil and dust filling the cabin. Abby settled into her usual spot, head on her paws, eyes half-closed but alert.

The livestream stayed on as the sun dipped low. Fifty viewers, then thirty, then back to forty. One of them typed, *Still here, Wolf. Keep walking.*

That was enough.

We stopped for a night in the parking lot of the Concordia Lutheran Church, where a supporter had arranged a stay for us. Gypsy and I walked into town, making our way through the streets and out toward the west side before circling back. A few people stopped to ask what we were about and seemed supportive, but most looked at us like we didn't belong—like lepers on parade. The stares stung more than I wanted to admit. By the time we made it back to the church lot, I felt like the message I carried had found deaf ears.

The next morning was Sunday. I decided to attend service at the church, partly out of respect, partly out of need. Partway through, as a visiting pastor spoke about his mission work overseas—how he fought to keep faith alive in a place where hope was running thin—I found myself wiping a tear from my eye. His words weren't about me, but somehow, they were exactly what I needed to hear.

The following day, we drove to Walden, Colorado, after following Highway 40 to 125. After a night there, we continued south on 14 toward Rustic, where we stayed at Glen Echo—a small RV and cabin retreat tucked deep in the Colorado Rockies. One of my supporters had rented us a spot, and once we'd set up camp, I took Abby down to the river. The white-capped rapids kicked up a cool, misty breeze as they tore past the rocks. I stood there for a long while, watching the current twist and foam, letting the sound wash through me and clear my head.

The next day, we drove through Fort Collins. I didn't get out to walk there. Something about Colorado felt different—colder somehow. Whenever I did step out to walk, I could feel eyes on me, and not the kind filled with curiosity or support. It felt like people were sneering, as if the flag I carried had become something to question instead of something to honor.

That night, we parked at the back of the lot behind Cornerstone Baptist Church in Windsor—the mountains behind us now, the plains unfolding ahead. The wind picked up, rocking *Beechy* just enough to remind us she was still alive.

One follower tracked us down there, wanting to meet in person and place his letter in the Grey Wolf Pony Express bag. Mr. T had gone to dinner with his daughter, so it was just me, Gypsy and the quiet hum of *Beechy's* generator when the night settled in.

Later, I sat at the dinette, the notebook open in front of me, the words spilling out slow and uneven:

The walk has changed. It's not about crowds anymore. It's about faith. It's about showing up when nobody else does.

Outside, the flag still fluttered in the wind, lit by the amber glow of a church parking-lot lamp. I thought about the people who'd stopped in Vernal—the mom, the boy, the oilfield worker. They were the reason I couldn't quit. Even if no one else was watching, God was.

Somewhere out in the dark, a trucker blew his horn twice—one long, one short. A freedom honk.
I smiled.

In the quiet that followed, I thought back to the day I'd left Carson City, full of vision and fire. I'd imagined a movement—thousands marching behind me, flags snapping in the wind, the kind of sight that would make the news ignore everything else.

But standing there in that empty church parking lot, I realized something I hadn't understood until then: —*movements don't always start with masses. Sometimes they start with a whisper in the wilderness. Sometimes they start with one man and a wounded shoulder still willing to walk.*

I looked out through *Beechy's* open door at the empty road, the faint red blink of taillights fading into distance. The world might not have been watching anymore, but I was still walking.

And as long as there was road ahead, I wasn't done yet.

Chapter 37 – The Long Plain

Morning broke soft and cool behind the Cornerstone Baptist Church, the flag outside snapping in a wind that carried the bite of changing seasons. The mountains were gone now, left behind like an old chapter—their jagged silhouettes traded for open sky and low fields that reached forever. I stood beside *Beechy*, coffee in hand, watching the light stretch across the plains. Abby sniffed the grass near the curb.

Mr. T stepped out, rubbing sleep from his eyes.

"East again?" he asked.

"East again," I said.

Then Gypsy emerged from the trailer, the chill of morning still clinging to his breath. He'd set up a cot inside, where he slept, and without a word began his morning ritual—setting up the camp stove beside *Beechy* and getting breakfast started. Sausage sizzled in the pan, eggs cracked against the rim, and diced potatoes hit the skillet with a soft hiss. The smell of grease and coffee mingled in the cool air— simple comforts that always felt like a luxury on the road.

We rolled out of Windsor just after sunrise, the sky brushed pink and gold. The air felt heavier, almost reluctant, as if even the wind wasn't sure it wanted to keep going. Highway signs pointed east toward Sterling, and I caught myself glancing at the fuel gauge more than usual. Out here, the miles didn't race by—they settled in. Long ribbons of asphalt unspooled ahead, the kind that make your mind wander farther than the wheels ever could.

That night, we parked in a Walmart lot on the edge of Sterling. The hum of semis idling in the distance blended with the occasional whistle of a train. It wasn't glamorous, but it was shelter—and in its own way, it was perfect. The next morning, we moved to the Sterling RV Park, a quiet spot tucked behind a row of cottonwoods—secured by one of the supporters who still checked in every day to help us along. Their generosity always hit the same way: unexpected, humbling, a reminder that even when the crowds thinned, faith still had its fingerprints all over the journey.

That evening, I walked a few miles through town with Gypsy at my side. People watched from their porches or cars. A few waved; a few didn't. I'd learned not to expect anything—just to walk, to wave, to keep showing up. A young man leaned out from a pickup at a stoplight.
"You some kind of preacher?" he called.
I laughed. *"Something like that!"*
He grinned and drove off. The light turned green, and the road opened again.

The next morning's livestream drew about fifty-eight viewers and a hundred and fourteen likes—a mix of old names and new ones scrolling across the chat, flickering in and out like passing headlights. Someone typed, *Still with you, Wolf. Keep walking.*
I smiled at the screen. Sometimes one message was enough to keep the miles moving.

We left Sterling after a couple of days, the road east rolling flat and straight beneath a pale sky. *Beechy* hummed steady, her engine finding its rhythm again after the mountain climbs. Abby curled up by my leg on the passenger seat. The prairie opened wide—a sea of gold and brown grass stretching farther than sight, the horizon drawn thin like a quiet dare.

By afternoon, we reached Holyoke—a small town folded into the middle of farmland. I streamed a short walk through its side streets, waving at the occasional passing truck. The sidewalks were clean, the air thick with the scent of cut hay. Not many people stopped, but a few honked their horns and gave thumbs-up. Small moments. Small reminders.

We pressed on toward Grant, Nebraska, crossing the state line just before sunset. There's something about crossing into Nebraska that feels like stepping into the country's open heart—the wide center where everything seems to breathe a little slower.

Then Mr. T glanced in the mirror and caught a thin trail of blue smoke curling from the trailer. We pulled to the shoulder and climbed out. The rear axle welds had broken clean through, and the tires were rubbing hard against the fender, throwing off that burnt-rubber smell that makes your stomach drop. We eased her forward about half a mile until we reached a farmhouse with a weathered barn and a gravel side road beside it. That's where we parked and took stock.

Discord was already hopping with supporters, and before long they'd tracked down a mobile welder—one willing to come all the way from across the Colorado line to get us back on the road.

As we approached Grant, one of *Beechy's* rear tires blew out. We limped her into town, hazard lights flashing, and found a small tire shop willing to take us in. The mechanic shook his head at the worn rubber, installed a new tire, and sent us on our way with a nod that said he'd seen it all before.

That night, we parked in Grant and I hosted a panel livestream with Dr. Pierre Kory—someone I'd first met during the convoy. He greeted me warmly, with the kind of respect that doesn't need explaining. We talked about faith, perseverance, and what it means to walk for something unseen. He spoke about the growing number of vaccine injuries he'd been witnessing, and I shared how far we'd come—and how far there still was to go. He listened closely, then said he'd join me for a few miles once I reached Illinois, if time permitted.

The stream drew more than five hundred views that night—the biggest audience I'd had in weeks. When it ended, I sat staring at the quiet screen, wondering why the same people who filled the chat weren't showing up along the road. Maybe the long silences, the slow miles, had grown dull to watch. Maybe the noise of the world had just gotten louder than the sound of one man walking.

I stayed there for a while, the glow of the screen fading to black, feeling lighter somehow—as if a bit of the old fire had flickered back to life.

The next morning, we drove east toward Gothenburg. The miles slid by quiet and smooth, telephone poles ticking past like the hands of a clock. We camped at the Lafayette Park RV Campground for the night.

At sunrise, Gypsy and I set out on foot toward the Pony Express Station in Gothenburg. Mr. T parked *Beechy* on the street just south of the small park where the station now stands, and I made sure the livestream was up and running. As I stepped through the doorway, the weight of the moment settled in—three hundred miles walked. Three hundred miles of flags, wind, faith, and footsteps.

The little log building sat quiet under the morning sun. Once, it had stood miles away along the Platte River, a way-station for riders trading out their tired horses before vanishing again into the plains. Years later, townsfolk moved it here to preserve what remained—a humble piece of history tucked between the trees.

I walked slowly around it, hand tracing the rough-hewn logs darkened by time, thinking about those riders and what it must have taken to keep going, not knowing if the next man down the line would even be waiting. In their day, messages were carried in leather pouches; mine traveled through cameras and screens. The tools had changed—but the mission, in its own way, hadn't.

I steadied the gimbal in my hand and let the camera pan across the park before turning it toward the old Pony Express Station. The morning light caught the weathered logs, their grain worn smooth by more than a century of wind and weather. Then I faced the lens.
"Three hundred miles," I said. *"The old Pony Express ran through here—carrying messages across America. I guess I'm still doing the same thing, just slower."*

For a moment, the only sound was the flag snapping in the breeze. Then the chat began to fill:

Still with you, Wolf.

Right on, brother.

Three hundred down—the Republic to go.

I smiled, lifted the flag on Wolfie a little higher, and said quietly, *"Let's keep going."*

We traveled to Lexington next—October now on the calendar—where we camped at the Dawson County Fairgrounds. Dot and Barb, supporters who'd been tracking me on the livestream and working with one of my moderators, opened the concession stand to feed us and anyone else who stopped by. The next morning, they joined me for a walk to Walmart and back to the campground. A few drivers called out, "God bless you!" as they passed. I waved and kept moving.

From Lexington, we rolled into Kearney and set up at the Buffalo County Fairgrounds. Later that evening, a familiar pickup pulled into camp—it was Dennis from the convoy. He was heading north and decided to stop by to see me and Mr. T.

The next morning, Dennis and Gypsy joined me for a walk into town. The rhythm of shoes on pavement felt good again—three men side by side, flags moving in sync. Later that afternoon, I did an interview at a local station, **KGFW** Radio—smaller than the one in Vernal, but just as welcoming. They asked the same questions I'd heard in town after town: Why walk? What does it mean?

My answers hadn't changed.

"It's about faith," I told them.

"It's about freedom. And it's about not waiting for someone else to fix what's broken."

Ron "Grey Wolf" Coleman at KGFW, Kearney, NE. — September 2022

When the interview wrapped, I thanked the host, shook her hand, and walked the miles back to camp.

The next day, after Dennis went on his way, Gypsy and I walked to Harvey Park to wait and see if anyone might show up for the meet-and-greet we'd announced on the radio the day before.
No one came.

By then, I'd grown used to it—empty parks, quiet streets, the wind carrying away the sound of my voice. Still, I showed up. Every mile was a kind of promise, even if no one else was there to see it kept.

Tires had become a recurring headache. We'd bent a rim back in Gothenburg, and not long after, blew a tire leaving the campground. We had it replaced there in town before leaving. Another replacement was ordered and shipped ahead to DeWitt, Nebraska, where we planned to stop next.

When we left Kearney, Mr. T drove *Beechy* to DeWitt to help a friend build a small porch and handicap ramp. It also gave us a chance to pick up the new tire that had been shipped there. From DeWitt, Gypsy and I took the replacement to a shop in Plymouth, had it mounted on *Beechy's* spare rim, and installed it—keeping the bent one as the backup. Then we pushed on toward Beatrice. Mr. T would meet back up with us a few days later once his work was done.

Gypsy and I carried on alone, the road running straight through open fields. The air turned cooler each morning, a whisper of fall riding the Nebraska wind. Somewhere ahead, the next chapter of the walk was waiting.

Chapter 38 – The Messenger's Weight

The air carried that faint crispness of mid-October — the kind that tells you summer's finally given up its hold.

We set up at the Chautauqua Park Tabernacle RV Park — a peaceful stretch of ground beneath a giant black-walnut tree. The squirrels didn't much appreciate our arrival. From sunrise to dusk they hurled walnuts down at *Beechy* like artillery fire, each one landing with a crack loud enough to make us laugh and duck. Inside, it sounded like someone dropping boulders on the roof. More than once I stepped on one and nearly rolled an ankle. *"Incoming!"* became the running joke of those days.

The campground sat just off the Big Blue River, the air rich with damp earth and the scent of falling leaves. It felt good to stop — to breathe again without counting miles. Gypsy and I spent one morning tidying up camp and another driving unhitched into town.

Beatrice was a quiet, old-style Midwestern city — brick storefronts, faded awnings, and stoplights hung sideways instead of vertical. Heads turned as we passed in *Beechy*, her flags rippling in the breeze. A few people pointed and smiled; others just stared, curious what the old rig represented.

We were on our way to have breakfast at the American Legion Hall. When we pulled into the parking lot, all eyes turned toward *Beechy* — she drew attention everywhere she went. Outside the entrance, a few patriots gathered, asking questions about the walk and the meaning behind the flag. Inside, the smell of bacon and coffee wrapped around us as we stood in line to pay the cashier before filling our plates. We found seats among the crowd, talking with several folks about freedom, liberty, and how easily both were being chipped away from the American people.

That evening, we returned downtown for a meet-and-greet organized by Ashley from the *Nebraska Against Government Overreach* group. Inside the small restaurant, the scent of fried food mingled with laughter and the low hum of conversation from the other diners. In the back room, double doors opened to the main dining area, where a few locals peeked in, curious about what was happening.

We made our way inside, weaving past tables and friendly faces. The chatter softened as I looked toward the back — and that's when I saw him.

A familiar face.

Steve Spurgeon — the musician and friend from our convoy days — stood near the doorway with that same easy grin. He was the man behind *Wake Up in the USA*, the anthem that carried the early miles of the Grey Wolf Walk. He greeted me with a firm handshake that said more than words ever could.

"Been a long road," he said.

"Still walking," I told him.

We sat together with a handful of others, talking about faith, the state of the country, and how Americans needed to find their courage again. Then Steve unzipped his guitar case and began to play.

First came *Wake Up in the USA* — familiar, resolute, the kind of song that could still raise goosebumps. Then he played a new one he'd just finished writing: *Let's Save America*. The chords rolled through the room like a prayer set to music. Even the clatter of dishes and laughter from the main dining area faded to silence. When he finished, there was a long, quiet moment — that rare stillness where everyone knows they've just witnessed something that matters.

We shook hands afterward, greeting a few folks who'd stopped by curious about the flags outside. It wasn't a crowd, but it didn't need to be. Sometimes a few voices in agreement carry farther than a stadium full of noise. Gypsy and I headed back to the campground under the walnut tree, the night wind cool and clean off the river.

The next afternoon, a white pickup truck pulled into the lot behind our trailer. It was Mr. T, back from DeWitt — tired but smiling after finishing his friend's ramp and porch. We stood outside talking for a while, the thud of falling walnuts punctuating the conversation.

A day later, my nephew James and his girlfriend drove down from the Omaha area. They brought supplies, a few dollars, hugs, and more encouragement than they probably realized. Their visit felt like a breath of home.

By week's end, *Beechy* was packed and ready again. We shared one last round of coffee beneath that walnut tree — dodging a final barrage from our squirrel neighbors — before rolling east toward St. Joseph, Missouri.

We drove straight through, arriving by evening and pulling into the Beacon RV Park a couple of miles from downtown. Early the next morning, I woke to the sound of voices outside. When I stepped out, I was met with a surprise that stopped me cold: parked directly behind *Beechy* was Jen M — one of my longtime moderators, supporters, and a friend from the second half of the convoy. She had driven up from Arkansas to surprise me — and she succeeded.

But she also had another mission: some important paperwork from home needed my signature and a notary's seal. We shared breakfast and coffee at the picnic table, catching up on the months since the convoy, laughing about the road, and planning the day ahead. Then Jen joined Gypsy and me for a walk to the Pony Express Museum, with Mr. T following behind in *Beechy*.

We spent hours there. The museum attendant, just opening for the morning, welcomed us warmly and encouraged us to take our time. The exhibits were small but powerful — weathered saddles, dispatch pouches, rifles, maps, and portraits of the riders who'd carried messages through storms and danger across the frontier. As I walked among them, I couldn't help but feel the parallel. They'd carried the words of a young nation. I was carrying its spirit — step by step, flag in hand, believing it still mattered.

Afterward, Jen M and I crossed the park to the giant steam locomotive resting on a short stretch of display track. We stood there staring at it, amazed by its sheer size. Later I'd learn they had actually laid temporary track into the park to move it there, then removed the rails afterward.

From there, we headed to the St. Joseph Public Library to have my documents signed and notarized — one of Jen M's official missions for the day. Once everything was stamped and sealed, she gathered the papers neatly and promised to mail them back to my daughter in Reno.

Our final stop was the Missouri State Highway Patrol station for an inspection on the trailer. We needed their approval so Jerry, the trailer's owner, could complete the registration and send us a new license plate. Two troopers came out to take a look. You could read the disbelief on their faces — *Beechy* idling out front, the homemade trailer hitched behind, both held together by equal parts steel and prayer.

They circled the rig, checking the hitch, tires, axles, and lights. Everything passed. One of them gave a low whistle.
"She's still running?" he asked.
I grinned. "She's got a few more miles in her yet."

The troopers laughed, signed the paperwork, and wished us safe travels. With that, Jen M's second task for the day was complete, and both sets of documents were ready to be mailed back to Reno.

When we returned to the campground, the smell of something home-cooked greeted us before we even stepped inside. Jen M had started an oven full of homemade comfort before leaving for the day — warm, hearty food that filled *Beechy* with the kind of peace only a home-cooked meal can bring. We ate inside, sharing stories and laughter late into the night.

The next morning, we hugged goodbye. As she drove off, I watched her taillights disappear down the road, feeling that familiar ache of gratitude — the kind that comes from knowing you're not walking this road alone.

As the morning light touched the trees, it struck me how fitting it was that all of this — the walk, the mission, the message — had led me here, to the birthplace of the Pony Express. Those riders once carried letters that stitched a nation together. I was still trying to do the same — one step, one voice, one mile at a time.

Chapter 39 – The Long Road to Hannibal

We left St. Joseph early, the sky still pale and bruised with dawn. *Beechy* rumbled steady beneath us as we pointed her nose east toward Hannibal, Missouri — a hundred ninety-three miles of open road ahead. The fields on either side were wide and empty, the highway stretching straight as an arrow through the heart of the state. Fence lines blurred past in silver morning light, and every so often a lone farmhouse stood against the horizon like a sentinel watching us pass.

By then, the walk had taken on a quieter rhythm. The livestreams had grown smaller, but the mission hadn't changed. I wasn't walking for numbers; I was walking for what I believed in — for the reminder that America's heartbeat still echoed in the hearts of ordinary people. The miles were fewer for a while, but the message stayed the same.

We reached Hannibal by midafternoon and set up camp at the Mark Twain Cave RV Park, tucked just south of town near the river. The people who worked there couldn't have been kinder. A few campers stopped to stare as *Beechy* pulled in — not because they recognized me, but because they couldn't believe a rig that old was still rolling. The flags flapping behind her drew even more attention. One man walking his dog stopped in his tracks and grinned. "Sixty-seven, huh?" he said, running a hand along the faded paint. "That's a survivor."

"Yeah," I told him. *"She's been through a lot. We both have."*

That night, the camp settled into its evening quiet — the smell of woodsmoke and barbecue drifting through the trees, the faint hum of the highway just far enough away to sound like the ocean. My moderators on Discord were busy at work. They'd found out there was an event happening in Hannibal that weekend — a fair and street gathering that drew big crowds. The plan was to set up a booth, a simple table where we could hand out freedom cards, pocket Constitutions, and talk to folks about what the walk stood for.

We waited to hear back on whether we'd get a space. In the meantime, I went live from camp, showing the Missouri hills behind us and talking about the road ahead. *"We've come a long way,"* I said into the camera. *"And we're not done yet."*

The next day passed slow but easy. Mr. T checked over *Beechy*, tightening bolts and topping off fluids while Gypsy cleaned the trailer and organized supplies. Near sunset, a golf cart rolled down the park road carrying a few locals making friendly rounds with the campers. They stopped by our site, waved, and one of them called out, "We're putting on a free concert tonight up at the winery—food, music, good people. You ought to come."

Mr. T and Gypsy decided to stay behind, but I went. It felt good to stretch my legs and be among people again. The winery sat on a small rise overlooking the river valley, lit by strings of white lights that swayed gently in the breeze. Inside, the air was thick with the smell of barbecue and sweet wine. I'm not much of a wine man, so I grabbed a plate of chicken wings and a soda, found a spot at a picnic table, and let the music roll through the night.

Before the band started, I struck up a few conversations — simple, honest talk about where I'd come from and why I was walking. Folks were kind, curious, and more than a few seemed genuinely moved. "Keep going," one woman said, resting her hand over her heart. "We need people like you out there."

The band took the stage soon after — a local group, full of energy and talent, the kind that plays for love more than money. They'd been the ones who invited me up, and between songs, one of them even mentioned the walk. "There's a man here tonight carrying a flag across America," she said into the mic. "Doing it for all the right reasons." The crowd clapped. I felt that old fire stir again.

Later, as I made my way back to camp, the night air was cool, the road quiet except for the occasional bark of a dog or chirp of crickets. I thought about how simple it was — that connection between strangers, the kind that reminded me why I'd started in the first place.

But the next morning brought frustration. My moderators had been up half the night working the phones, trying to secure that booth at the Hannibal event. What should've been a routine arrangement turned into something else entirely. The organizer, a local woman in charge of vendor spaces, refused to approve it. No real reason — just "No." My team tried to reason with her, even contacted the mayor's office and the chamber of commerce. The replies were polite, but the tone was clear: **we'd been shut out.**

Word spread through our Discord chat, and anger rippled through the community. Some called it censorship, others said it was just politics. Maybe it was both. I didn't want to feed the negativity, but I couldn't ignore the truth either — patriotism had become something controversial. The same flag that once united people now made some recoil.

Steve Spurgeon heard about it too. He posted a message online, calling out the organizer's comments that had surfaced through mutual acquaintances and social media. He defended the walk, defended me, and reminded everyone that standing for freedom shouldn't need anyone's permission. His words meant a lot. Steve had always been one of the good ones — honest, steady, rooted in faith and conviction.

We stayed four days in Hannibal, waiting, hoping something might change. It didn't. We decided to move on. Sometimes the best way to fight a closed door is to keep walking past it.

When we pulled out of Mark Twain Cave RV Park that morning, the river mist clung to *Beechy's* sides. I looked back once at the little town on the hill — Hannibal, the boyhood home of Mark Twain, the storyteller of America's restless spirit. I couldn't help but think: *he'd understand this journey.*

We headed south on Highway 61, the "Avenue of the Saints." The plan was simple: fuel up in New London, then continue toward St. Louis. The day was bright and crisp, the kind that makes even hardship feel bearable. But about ten miles outside of town, things took a turn.

Mr. T pulled into a Love's station to fuel up. *Beechy* came to a stop, and the familiar clatter of her old engine went silent. When Mr. T turned the key again, nothing — not even a click. The battery was dead. He looked over at me through the windshield and mouthed a single word: "Great."

We fired up *Beechy's* generator, switched the system to back-charge the chassis batteries, and waited. A few minutes later she roared to life, but the relief was short-lived — the alternator wasn't charging. We limped her to the side of the lot and shut her down. Mr. T grabbed a flashlight, and popped the engine cover. The smell of burnt insulation and old oil hit us both.

"Alternator's shot," he said, tapping it with a wrench. "We're dead in the water until we get a new one."

I went inside and spoke with the manager, explaining our situation. The staff couldn't have been more accommodating, letting us stay parked in the lot until we could get parts. I called a few auto shops nearby, found one that said they had the right alternator, and arranged for delivery. When it arrived, Mr. T opened the box — wrong model. Close, but no fit.

Back on Discord, my supporters jumped into action again, combing through parts stores across three states. That's when Jen M — my steadfast moderator and friend from the convoy — chimed in. "I found it," she said. "Same part number, right brand, in stock near me."

She was in Arkansas. Nearly six hours away.

"I'll drive it to you," she added. "Don't move."

The next day, just past noon, a familiar little pickup rolled into the lot. Jen stepped out, holding the box like it was made of gold. "I come bearing gifts," she said with a grin.

My left shoulder by then was almost useless, the pain sharp enough to take my breath away whenever I moved wrong. But seeing her brought a surge of relief that dulled everything else. Mr. T unboxed the new alternator, compared it to the original, and nodded. "That's the one."

He got to work right there in the lot, tools spread across the floor. Within an hour, *Beechy* was humming again — charging strong, running better than she had in weeks. We boxed up the incorrect part and gave it to Jen to return on her way home.

Before she left, she looked me straight in the eye and said, "You need to get that shoulder looked at. I'm taking you down to the VA hospital in St. Louis. No arguments."

I didn't argue. I couldn't. The pain had reached a point where sleep was almost impossible. Even holding Wolfie during livestreams had become agony. So we made a plan. Mr. T and Gypsy would head toward St. Louis in the morning to meet us at a truck stop, while Jen drove me down that night to finally get some answers.

Mr. T and Gypsy stayed behind at the Love's in New London, parking *Beechy* for the night. By morning, they'd roll south toward St. Louis to meet us.

After my visit to the emergency room, my supporters had already arranged a hotel room for me, and Jen drove me there before heading to her mother's house just north of town. I was completely deflated. The ER doctor had taken X-rays, glanced at them, and told me it was just bursitis. He handed me a tube of ointment that smelled like Ben-Gay and said to take Tylenol. That was it.

I knew better. I knew something was truly wrong.

Back in the hotel room, I sat on the edge of the bed, opened my laptop, and started researching the upcoming midterm elections. If I couldn't move forward physically, I could at least stay informed— understand what was coming, what it all might mean for the mission.

We weren't done yet, but I could feel something shifting.
The road ahead wasn't just about endurance anymore.
It was about facing what was breaking—both in my body and in my country—and finding a way to keep moving anyway.

Chapter 40 – The Weight of the Republic

Morning came slow and gray through the hotel curtains. My shoulder throbbed like a live wire under my skin, each movement sending a dull ache through the rest of me. Jen picked me up a little after sunrise, and we walked to a small diner just down the street. The place smelled of bacon grease and coffee—the kind of scent that anchors you to the world when everything else feels like it's coming apart.

A couple at the next table struck up a conversation. I told them about the walk, the flag, and what it all meant. Even here—in a big city where most folks seemed lost in their own storms—there was still curiosity, still that spark of recognition. We talked for a while, and I could see it in their eyes: they understood, at least a little, what I was trying to do. For a few minutes, the noise of the world outside faded, replaced by that quiet connection that only truth can bring.

After breakfast, Jen and I walked the several blocks to where she'd parked. I enjoyed walking with her. Back home, she ran every day—marathons, even—so keeping pace with me was nothing. She was the one who'd been in my ear at the start of this journey, coaching me on breathing, pacing, conserving energy for the long miles ahead.

We drove to the truck stop on the outskirts of St. Louis, where Mr. T and Gypsy had arrived earlier that morning. *Beechy* sat parked beneath the wide sky, her flags rippling in the morning breeze. Mr. T looked tired but managed a smile when he saw us. Gypsy had caught a bus into town to pick up a new pair of shoes and a jacket.

Before heading north to visit her parents, Jen insisted on taking me shopping at Walmart to restock supplies. I didn't argue. I was worn thin—body and spirit—and it felt good to let someone else take the lead for a while.

When we returned to the truck stop after shopping, we unpacked the groceries and supplies inside *Beechy*, then set up our camp chairs out front. For a while, we just sat and talked—reminiscing about the convoy days, the early miles of the walk, and what might come next once the road finally ended. The hum of idling trucks filled the pauses between stories.

After an hour or so, Jen stood, brushed the road dust from her pants, and said her goodbyes. There were hugs all around, and then I watched as her little pickup eased out of the lot and disappeared into traffic. The quiet that followed settled deep.

That night, the truck stop didn't sleep. Sirens howled through the dark, and the crack of gunfire echoed somewhere too close to ignore. I stared at the ceiling of *Beechy*, thinking about how far we'd come—and how far I might still have to go.

At dawn, we rolled out, eager to leave the noise behind. The road east carried us across the Mississippi and into Illinois. Sixty-odd miles later, we pulled into Vandalia, a town steeped in history and quiet pride. We parked in the Walmart lot, and I knew what I needed to do next.

The next morning, Gypsy and I walked from the lot down to the Old Statehouse—the first capitol of Illinois, where a young Abraham Lincoln had once served as a legislator. My arm was still bound in a sling, but I carried my walking stick—Wolfie—with the flag I'd rescued on the very first day of the walk tie-wrapped to it. The livestream was rolling, and the chat filled with words of encouragement as we made our way through the quiet streets of Vandalia.

Inside, the air smelled of old wood and varnish. The creak of the stairs beneath my shoes felt like stepping back through time. Plaques on the walls told the story of the men who'd shaped the state—and in many ways, the nation. I paused beside the wax figure of Lincoln, his face lit soft by the morning sun filtering through high windows.

"Imagine," I told the camera, *"the kind of courage it took to stand for what you believed in when the whole world wanted you quiet."*

I climbed the stairs to the second floor, each step groaning under the weight of its own history. At the landing, I paused and turned to Gypsy. *"Just think,"* I said. *"We're walking on the same steps Abraham Lincoln once walked—the same creak of the boards, the same echoes in the air."*

In the Senate chamber, I stood where Lincoln had once spoken and let the moment settle. The room felt suspended in time—wood polished by generations, sunlight slanting through tall windows, dust motes drifting like quiet witnesses. I thought about the distance between his time and ours—how fragile the republic still was, how easily liberty could slip away if people stopped guarding it.

Wax Figure of Abraham Lincoln in Vandalia State House Museum, Vandalia, IL. — October 2022

When the tour ended, Gypsy and I walked outside, crossed the street, and stopped beside a bronze statue of Lincoln sitting on a bench. I sat down beside him for a photo, half smiling at the symbolism—the man who saved the Union, and the man trying to remind the Union what it still stood for.

Afterward, Gypsy said he wanted to run a few errands and would meet me back at *Beechy*. So I started the long walk from the Statehouse back to the Walmart lot, the livestream rolling the entire way.

As I walked, I spoke about freedom—about what Lincoln had stood for, not only as a state legislator but as the nation's first Republican president. A man who led through a war that nearly tore the country apart and who paid for his convictions with his life. His courage, his faith in the Constitution, his belief that a divided nation could still be made whole—those were the same ideals that had carried me across every mile of this walk.

That evening, supporters arranged for us to move to the Dragon RV Park just down the road. It was a quiet place—one I knew we'd be calling home for a while. I still needed answers from the VA. Reno had arranged for an MRI in St. Louis, and the next day Mr. T drove me back to the city.

The results came quickly, but they were useless. The disc they gave me held only a single chart—no images, no real data. After a few tense calls, the VA promised to overnight a corrected copy. Days passed. Two weeks, nearly, spent in Vandalia, waiting, healing, thinking.

When the new MRI finally arrived, the radiologist's report said "no significant findings." I knew that wasn't right. One of my supporters reached out to an orthopedic surgeon in Terre Haute, Indiana—a patriot who agreed to see me, no insurance, just a handshake and a small fee.

We left the trailer locked up at camp and made the trip. The doctor examined my shoulder carefully, watched how the pain flared when I tried to move. Then he looked me in the eye and said, "Congratulations —you've got a locked, frozen shoulder."

He had already reviewed the MRI from the DVD I'd handed to the receptionist on my way in.
"There's more going on in there than they told you," he said. "You'll need surgery. You've got a bone spur pressing on a nerve, and your labrum's in rough shape."

Before I left, he gave me a steroid injection—temporary relief, maybe a few weeks at best. I thanked him, paid the hundred dollars we'd agreed on, and made the long drive back to Vandalia, the pain dulled but the truth of his words heavy on my mind.

That night, *Beechy's* lights glowed soft against the cold Illinois dark. I sat at the dinette, the sling cradling my arm, and wrote in my notebook:

Even when the body breaks, the mission can't.

Faith is the part that doesn't fracture.

The November elections were underway, and it looked as though the Republican Party would take the majority in both the House of Representatives and the Senate. I started thinking practically about the mission.

In my heart, I had always pictured it differently—thousands of people stretching for miles behind me, a human tide moving together toward Washington, D.C., like a living, breathing banner of freedom. The mainstream media wouldn't have been able to ignore that. But that vision hadn't come to pass.

And the truth was, even if I made it all the way to D.C., it wouldn't move the needle now. The current Congress was a lame duck; anything said or done before January would fall on deaf ears until the 118th Congress was sworn in.

Those thoughts weighed heavy, along with the doctor's words back in Terre Haute—you'll need surgery. Maybe it was time to go home. Not to quit the mission, but to regroup, recover, and prepare for what came next.

We rolled east into Effingham, Illinois, and set up camp at the Petro truck stop. The weather had turned bitterly cold, snow dusting the parking lot one evening. Over the next few days, I did a lot of thinking.

Then came a reminder of the family forged on this road. Friends from the convoy rolled in—Truckingirl and Richard, Lil Blinky and Miss Kay, Eric and Polish Agnes. Blinky arrived with a spread fit for an army: fried chicken, mashed potatoes, biscuits, and corn. We feasted right there in the parking lot, laughing, sharing stories, and shaking off the cold.

By the next morning, they were gone again—each heading back to their own battles, their own miles. I stood there in the crisp Illinois air, the lot empty now except for *Beechy*, and knew what came next.

We would go no farther east.

We would turn west—Reno bound.

Chapter 41 – The Long Road Home

We left Effingham before sunrise, the world still half-asleep under a skin of frost. *Beechy's* engine rumbled low and steady, a sound that had become as familiar as my own heartbeat. We were heading west—Reno bound. The decision was made, but it carried weight. Every mile would now measure both distance and reckoning: what had been done, what remained undone, and what still lived in the space between.

Mr. T took the wheel while I sat wrapped in my coat at the dinette, Gypsy in the passenger seat, a mug of coffee warming my hands. *Beechy's* old heater hadn't worked in months, so we did what we always did— improvise, adapt, overcome.

Back in Salt Lake City, we'd been given hundreds of burlap sacks, and we'd put them to use—stuffing them around the freshwater tank to keep it from freezing, under the dash, and around the driver's compartment to block the drafts. Blankets layered every surface. An extra one lay across Mr. T's lap as he drove, his breath clouding in the cold morning air.

We ran a small electric heater off *Beechy's* generator and kept her old propane space heater roaring full blast. It wasn't comfort, but it was survival. Abby curled beside me, a small bundle of warmth and steady companionship in the bitter morning chill.

The highway unspooled straight and empty. Frost glimmered on the grass along the shoulders, telephone poles ticking by in a rhythm that matched the hum of *Beechy's* tires. I watched the horizon brighten from gray to rose, then to gold. The sky always seemed to forgive before the land did.

Traffic thinned as we crossed into Nebraska. The landscape stretched wide and clean, farms and windbreaks giving way to long sweeps of open prairie. Out there, the wind had its own voice—low, endless, and true.

I thought about how far we'd come: *from the deserts of Nevada, through the mountains and plains, through faith and pain and a thousand conversations about freedom.* The walk had changed shape, but not purpose. It was never just about endurance—it was about awakening something sleeping in the soul of America.

By late afternoon the sky had turned the color of pewter. We pulled into a rest area near Lincoln and ate sandwiches from the cooler. Mr. T checked the oil and coolant while I scrolled through messages from supporters. Some had drifted away since I'd announced we were heading home, but others stayed. They understood the truth: *that sometimes retreat isn't surrender—it's regrouping.*

That night, the temperature plunged. Inside *Beechy*, we could see our breath hang in the air like smoke. I woke several times, the pain in my shoulder flaring with every shift. Around four in the morning, I gave up on sleep, pulled on my jacket, and stepped outside. The stars over Nebraska burned cold and brilliant—each one a mile marker in reverse, pointing home.

Before we made it out of the state, climbing a small incline, a sudden roar echoed from beneath *Beechy's* doghouse cover. The sound was sharp, metallic—an exhaust manifold had cracked clean through, and the noise was deafening. I called my daughter in Reno and guided her to a dusty box on a shelf in my garage—the spare manifold I'd stashed there years earlier. She found it, boxed it up, and overnighted it to us.

We limped *Beechy* into a small roadside motel and shut her down for the night, waiting for the morning delivery. When the part arrived, we swapped it out in the parking lot—frozen fingers, stiff bolts, a few scraped knuckles—but she roared back to life before noon.

The next morning, we fueled up and pushed west again, *Beechy's* old 318-cubic-inch engine grumbling with every climb. By midday, we'd crossed into Wyoming, where the land turned harsh and beautiful—rolling plains rising into the first reach of the Rockies. Snow flurries swept across the highway, thin and silver, like whispers of what was still ahead.

Thanksgiving approached as we neared Cheyenne. We'd been running almost nonstop for two days, stopping only for fuel and coffee. The plan had been to find a warm place for the holiday, but plans on the road rarely hold. When we reached the TravelCenters of America truck stop on the edge of town, the parking lot was full of rigs, cars, and families. Inside, the smell of roasted turkey and cinnamon greeted us like a memory.

We stood in line with ranchers, truckers, and travelers who had all decided to spend the day here. The diner was packed—laughing kids, tired drivers, old couples holding hands across Formica tables. When our plates arrived—real turkey, mashed potatoes, green beans, and pumpkin pie—it felt like grace itself. For an hour we were just Americans at a Thanksgiving table, sharing food instead of headlines.

After dinner, Mr. T, Gypsy and I sat quietly for a while, letting the warmth soak in. "Guess this is home for the day," Mr. T said, smiling tiredly.

"Could be worse," I answered. *"Could be anywhere else."*

Outside, the wind had picked up, carrying snow across the lights of the truck stop. *Beechy* waited, patient as always, her sides flecked with road dust and pride. We climbed aboard and settled in for the night.

The next morning, the air was sharp enough to bite. Mr. T fired up *Beechy* and let her idle until the old engine found its rhythm, the exhaust puffing white against the frozen dawn. We ducked into the diner for breakfast and coffee—steam rising from our cups, the clatter of plates a brief comfort before the road.

Afterward, I walked Abby around the lot, her breath forming quick little clouds in the cold. Then we climbed aboard and turned west again.

The climb out of Cheyenne was brutal. Snow fell in hard, slanting sheets, and *Beechy* groaned with every mile. Her wipers scraped against the glass, struggling to keep up, while the wind howled through every seam and crack in her frame. Mr. T gripped the wheel with both hands, his eyes fixed on the faint red glow of taillights disappearing into the white.

I sat beside him, counting the miles to Laramie under my breath—small prayers between each one. We made it over Mt. Sherman and through Laramie.

Somewhere near Elk Mountain, the sky opened up—sunlight spilling across drifts of white, the world gleaming like glass. We pulled over at a scenic turnout and stepped outside. The silence was absolute, broken only by the ticking of the engine as it idled. "You think she'll make it home?" Mr. T asked, nodding toward *Beechy*.

"She's made it this far," I said. "So have we."

From there, it was on to Rawlins, then Rock Springs. We stopped for the night at Little America, had dinner, and by morning we were back on the road again. Then came Fort Bridger—snow still clinging to the hills, the air thin and sharp with altitude.

Each stop felt like a small victory, one more step closer to home. We'd fix what we could, rest, and then roll on.

Near Salt Lake City, though, trouble found us again. *Beechy's* rear main seal began to leak badly, oil dripping fast enough that we kept spare quarts stacked in cases in her rear compartment. Then, on that same stretch of highway, the alternator mount cracked clean through. We limped into a parts store outside the city, hoping for a miracle, but no one had the bracket we needed.

So I did what I always did—made do. I rigged a fix with two stainless-steel clamps and a prayer. It wasn't pretty, but it held.

We limped westward, every vibration sounding like a countdown. Past the salt flats, through Wendover, into the long emptiness of northern Nevada. The desert welcomed us with that familiar mix of beauty and cruelty—icy wind slicing across open ground, sky stretching wider than reason. *Beechy* moved steady, her old bones groaning but unbroken.

We stopped for the night in Wells, Nevada—at the Petro truck stop off the interstate. It felt strange being back in Nevada, like coming full circle, only older, wiser, and more worn. The cold here was familiar, the kind that cuts clean but somehow feels like home.

Inside the diner, the air smelled of coffee and diesel, the low hum of conversation wrapping around the clink of silverware. A waitress paused when she saw the flag pin on my jacket.

"You're that walking guy, right?" she asked.

I nodded, caught off guard.

"Saw you on Facebook months back," she said, smiling.

238

"Glad you made it this far."

That simple moment meant more than she probably knew.

The next day, Mr. T took the wheel through Winnemucca and on to Mill City while I rested my shoulder, grateful for the steady hum of the road beneath us. By afternoon, we switched—it was my turn to bring her home.

The sun dipped low behind the Sierra Nevada, painting the clouds in copper and crimson. Every mile westward smelled a little more like home. We had to make it by six; I was scheduled for an interview on Lindell TV about the rising cost of diesel fuel. We hit Reno at 5:45 p.m., just enough time for me to dash inside, set up my iPad, and join the broadcast. The questions came fast, but my mind kept drifting to the sound of *Beechy* cooling in the driveway.

When the interview ended, I hugged my family, then stepped outside into the chill evening air. The city lights flickered against the foothills, and *Beechy* waited in the drive, her paint dusted with miles of road. For the first time in months, there was no next destination—only home.

Something in me finally let go—a knot of exhaustion and relief that had carried through every mile. Abby barked once, sharp and happy, as if she knew. We were home.

Home.

That word carried a different weight now. It wasn't just a place—it was a pause, a promise, and maybe a beginning.

Within days I was back in the VA hospital. My primary-care physician had fast-tracked an appointment with an orthopedic surgeon. I handed the same DVD I'd carried from St. Louis to the receptionist and asked that it be uploaded to my chart. This time, they actually did it.

When the surgeon entered the exam room, he had already reviewed the images.
"You don't have a torn rotator cuff," he said, "but you do have a mess in there — a bone spur pressing on a nerve bundle and damage around the labrum. You'll need surgery."

He paused, then glanced at the second chart on his clipboard. "And the MRI on your knee shows a torn meniscus," he added. "That'll need surgery too — one thing at a time."

I nodded, half relieved, half angry — relieved that someone finally believed me, angry that two other doctors had dismissed the pain as nothing more than bursitis. He scheduled the shoulder surgery for February and said that with time and therapy I'd regain full use of the arm. The knee surgery would follow in July.

We'd taken Gypsy to the Greyhound station so he could head off to his next mission. Mr. T — my faithful companion through every mile — accepted my invitation to stay on as my roommate.

The weeks that followed blurred together in a mix of appointments, livestreams, and reflection. I spent long hours in my small home office, *Beechy* parked outside under the Nevada sun, her paint dulled by the miles but proud all the same. Viewers tuned in faithfully as I shared updates—about the journey, the lessons from the road, and the America I'd seen up close.

I told them that the walk had never been about crowds or cameras. It was about a covenant: *faith, freedom, and the soul of the Republic.* I still believed that with everything in me.

February came, and with it the surgery. The doctor later told me it had been tougher than expected—scar tissue, inflammation, bone spurs, even a partial labrum repair. "We had to break it free," he said. "You'll hurt for a while, but it'll heal right." He was right. The pain was sharp at first, but there was something clean about it—pain that meant progress instead of defeat.

Rehab was slow. Some days the arm felt like dead weight, others like proof that I was still in the fight. Between therapy sessions, I followed the news out of Washington. Bills were moving again—legislation that mirrored the objectives I'd carried across the country. One sought to repeal the lingering state of emergency; another to limit executive overreach. For months, I'd written emails, letters, and follow-ups to congressional offices, doing what I could to keep those issues alive.

Then, in early May—on my birthday—the news broke.

The President had signed the bill ending the national state of emergency.

I sat back in my chair, stunned for a moment. After all the miles, the storms, the doubters, and the silence—one of the very objectives that had launched the Grey Wolf Walk was finally complete. My first thought wasn't celebration; it was gratitude. Gratitude for every supporter who had believed when others turned away, for every prayer whispered on the roadside, for every mile that had carried me to that moment.

I opened a livestream that afternoon, arm still stiff from therapy, flag propped behind me. *"Well,"* I said, smiling into the camera, *"it looks like the mission kept walking even when I stopped."* Messages flooded in—cheers, emojis, prayers, tears. For a few minutes, the community that had carried me across a continent felt alive again.

When the stream ended, I sat quietly, watching the sun sink behind Red Peak. The desert light stretched long and golden across *Beechy's* front. She'd earned her rest. So had I.

I thought back to that first day in Carson City—the morning prayer, the first step east, the uncertainty and faith mingled in equal measure. None of it had gone according to plan, yet somehow it had all led here. The road, it seemed, always knows where it's going, even when we don't.

That night I wrote in my journal:

Freedom isn't a finish line. It's a duty renewed each day by those willing to carry it forward. Sometimes you march. Sometimes you crawl. Sometimes you drive an old RV held together by prayer. But you keep going.

I closed the book, turned off the light, and whispered a quiet thank-you to God, who had carried me through every mile. The battle for liberty would go on—it always does—but one chapter had finally found its end.

What a birthday present that was.

Epilogue

This journey was never about a convoy or a walk. It was about a calling.

Long before the first truck rolled or the first step hit the pavement, I knew something deep in my spirit: America was losing sight of herself.

The Founding Fathers built a republic — a government run by the people, not a people ruled by government. Somewhere along the way, that truth began to fade.

The road became my classroom, and the miles became my ministry. From the deserts of Nevada to the farmlands of Indiana, I met Americans who still believed — men and women who hadn't given up on this country, even when it felt like the country had given up on them. Their words, their tears, and their hope became the heartbeat of my mission.

Each flag waving from an overpass, each handshake, each story shared along the way reminded me that we the people still hold the power to steer this nation's course. But that power only lives if we remember how to use it.

What I learned is simple, but it changes everything: Freedom isn't granted — it's guarded. It isn't restored by politicians — it's renewed by patriots. Every generation must reclaim it, or risk watching it slip away.

My journey — my movement — has always been about that awakening. About standing in the gap between comfort and courage, and reminding Americans that our republic still belongs to us.

If you've read this far, maybe you feel that same stirring — that quiet conviction that something greater is calling you to stand, to speak, to act. Listen to it. That's the voice of liberty itself, and it's waiting for all of us to answer.

So I'll keep rolling, in whatever way I can — because this fight isn't about roads or rallies. It's about the soul of a nation.

And she's still worth every mile.

— Grey Wolf

Thanks

To the American people—the true owners of this Republic—thank you for reminding me what we're fighting for.

To those who stood on bridges, prayed on roadsides, waved flags, and shouted encouragement as we rolled past—you proved that the spirit of this nation still burns bright.

To every volunteer, organizer, driver, veteran, and supporter who carried the torch when others stayed silent—you are the reason this movement lives on.

To my friends, admins, and moderators—the extended family who worked tirelessly behind the scenes—your faith, your strength, and your courage gave this mission its voice.

To those who shared your stories of loss, sacrifice, and hope along the way—you reminded me that this journey was never about one man, but about all of us finding our way back home to the America our Founders envisioned.

And to my family—blood and chosen—thank you for your patience, your belief, and your love through every mile and every trial.

May God bless you all.
And may God bless the United States of America—land of the free, because of those who still dare to stand.

About the Author

Ron Coleman is a U.S. Air Force veteran, engineer, and long-haul truck driver whose life has spanned the heart of America's working class. Born and raised in Nevada, Ron learned early the values of hard work, faith, and country.

His professional career began in the early 1980s in telecommunications, where he built and managed long-distance switching centers, microwave systems, and global data networks. Over more than two decades, he rose to Vice President of Operations and Engineering for multiple companies, leading teams across the U.S. and abroad.

In time, Ron traded the boardroom for the open highway. Behind the wheel of his Kenworth, he rediscovered the country he had once served —its vast landscapes, its people, and its quiet resilience. Those miles became more than work; they became both a classroom and a calling.

As the world changed, Ron became a witness to the struggles of ordinary Americans—business owners, farmers, veterans, and families —each one fighting to hold on to freedom and dignity. His journey through The People's Convoy and his cross-country *Grey Wolf Walk Across America for Freedom* were not just acts of protest, but missions to carry the voices of those who felt forgotten.

Today, Ron continues to write and speak about liberty, faith, and the enduring American spirit. His story isn't about politics—it's about conviction, truth, and one man's journey to remind America of who she truly is.

Now retired, Ron lives in Nevada and still finds peace behind the wheel from time to time, taking on local trucking jobs. Each sunrise over the asphalt reminds him why he rolls—for faith, for freedom, and for the people.

 Also by Ron Coleman

Liberty & the Ink Well

A guided journey through America's founding ideals, this book
blends storytelling, historical insight, and personal reflection to help
readers rediscover the principles that shaped our nation.
Whether used for study, journaling, or inspiration, *Liberty & the Ink
Well* invites readers to engage deeply with the values that define
American freedom.

Grey Wolf Press
An Independent American Publisher
GreyWolfPress.net